T0355582

Nadine Olonetzky

INSPIRATIONS

TIME TRAVEL
THROUGH
GARDEN HISTORY

Birkhäuser
Basel

*This book is dedicated to the blackbird
who chose the olive tree on our balcony to build her nest in spring 2017.
She laid four eggs and raised the chicks with her mate.*

In the beginning there was green: without bushes, trees and flowers we couldn't breathe, couldn't live. Composing them into a garden allows them to grow further, beyond their pure use. Gardens bring together nature, people and art. The idea of the garden is one of paradise, not wilderness.

Inspirations – Time Travel through Garden History tells the story of the garden's development from its conjectured beginnings in Mesopotamia to the present day. The most important styles, trends and people in the art of the garden are presented in chronologically arranged segments with a focus on Central Europe. This journey through history is also meant to show how desires and world views give rise to new gardens, and gardens inspire artworks.

Every garden speaks to all of the senses: birds chirp in spring and fly busily from shrub to tree. In the summer one has the scent of freshly mowed grass in the morning; in autumn, that of fallen fruit. Eating raspberries right off the bush is an experience one remembers forever. The colours of self-grown carrots and flowers shine directly into the heart. And in winter, when it snows, everything is still, covered in white; the plants rest and gather strength for a fresh start in spring.

Even though famous, trendsetting gardens are often made possible by great wealth, beautiful gardens are not a privilege of the rich. Whether allotment, landscape or public park, cottage garden or balcony or community garden in the city – small and large gardens are interwoven throughout the built landscape and perhaps have more importance now than ever before in their history. In times of dense structures, gardens let us catch a breath of fresh air – in a broader sense – and for a great number of animals, they provide living spaces and a source of nourishment.

But why do raspberries taste like raspberries? Where do berries, fruit, vegetables and herbs get their taste if not from the soil of the garden, which contains an entire universe of life, and from the air, the rain, the sunlight and the heat?

Those who grow a garden create their own paradise. The literal taking root of bushes, trees and flowers in a garden and the flow of seasons offer a sense of constancy and stability. Gardens teach us to live in the moment, to perceive our surroundings with all of our senses and to reflect on what's essential. Not solely purpose and work, but delight and contemplation: gardens have utopian power as imagined spaces of happiness. Both the splendid historical garden as well as the small, idealistically nourished garden paradise bestow magic and poetry on the places we inhabit. Gardens are founded on ideas. Ideas grow in gardens.

Nadine Olonetzky

Paradise is a garden:
Lucas Cranach the Elder, *The Golden Age*, ca. 1530 →

PARADISE, from the Avestan word "pairí-daeza", composed of "roundabout" and "wall". Ubiquitous idea envisioning a place of tranquillity and peace where humankind wants for nothing. According to Genesis 2.8–13, paradise is the primordial home of humans and a fruitful garden with the Tree of Life, the Tree of Knowledge as well as the paradisiacal rivers Phison, Geon, Tigris, and Euphrates.

GARDEN, from Old High German "garto", also "gards", for "courtyard", "house", "family"; English "yard". Derived from the Indo-Germanic word "ghor-to-s": "wattle", "fence", "enclosure". The garden is the enclosed property in the proximity of the house. A garden is a garden because it is protected from the wilderness by a fence.

PARK, from Middle Latin "parricus": "enclosure", "fenced-off space", "game parks", or "wooded area". A large, partially forested garden; and for cities today, also a green belt. In addition to palace grounds and spa gardens, zoos and public and city parks, the word is also used for ensembles unrelated to a garden, such as technology, multimedia and office parks.

CHRONICLE OF GARDEN CULTURE

CIRCA 10 000 BC: DOMESTICATION In an arched area in the north of the Arabian peninsula, the so-called "Fertile Crescent", humans domesticate animals and plants for the first time – or at least when settled for the season in the area of the Euphrates. It is still too early to speak of a garden in the true sense of the word. Gardening or *horticulture* is carried out in an enclosed piece of land; agriculture, on fields in the open countryside.

CIRCA 4000 BC: THE GARDEN OF EDEN The steppes and deserts of Mesopotamia are considered the cradle of garden culture: the heat of the sun, the dry, rocky landscape inspire people to dream of trees that offer shade, of cooling fountains, flowers and fruit running with juice. The Sumerians begin to artificially irrigate the "land between the rivers" Euphrates and Tigris and to enclose hunting grounds and fig palm orchards. Domesticating wild plants and importing plant and animal species that are foreign to the region are revolutionary ideas. The Sumerian word "edin" means "fertile or irrigable land". At the time when the Book of Genesis was recorded by scribes (circa 10th to 6th century BC), the *Garden of Eden* is not only situated in Mesopotamia; the Jewish calendar begins with the creation of the world in 3761 BC, and therefore also at the time when the Sumerians made Mesopotamia fertile. The Hebrew word "gan eden" means "garden of well-being and pleasure". The Hebrew word "pardes" has the same root as the ancient Persian "pairí-daeza" – "paradise". PaRDeS is an acronym for the classical exegesis of the Tanakh (the Torah and other Jewish scriptures): every letter signifies a level of interpretation. The Tanakh, in turn, is found in the Christian Bible as the Old Testament. Henceforth, all three monolithic world religions link the image of the ideal world with a garden.

FROM 4000 BC: USE AND PLEASURE I Gardens depicted on papyrus scrolls and murals in the tombs of Egyptian dignitaries are testimony of a highly developed garden culture in the era of the

Ancient Kingdom. In the Nile Valley, Nile Delta and in the Faijum basin, tomb gardens are established around pyramids; more gardens are created in the temple districts and pleasure as well as vegetable gardens are planted. Due to the irrigation methods, they are rectangular in plan; they are also walled to protect against flooding from the Nile. Partially terraced, they feature trees planted at regular intervals, which also create internal divisions. Many gardens boast (fish-) ponds at the centre, with flowers growing along the edge and a pergola with grapevines.

On the one hand, the garden provides for existential needs by offering nourishment; on the other hand, it offers prestige and good fortune even beyond life on earth to the affluent sectors in society: "For you wander at leisure along the beautiful shore of your pond; your heart rejoices at your trees and is refreshed in the shade of your sycamores; your heart is content with the water from your well, which you have created to last for ever and eternity", reads a tomb inscription.

The gardens are moreover associated with religious ideas. Various deities are guarantors of fertility and renewal and are based in the garden, for example, Hathor, the goddess of joy, love, dance and music, also venerated as the goddess of trees.

Vegetable gardens are laid out in several square sections surrounded by small earth walls of roughly 40 cm in length. The commercial garden, the remnants of which were discovered south of Tell el-Amarna, is proof that the same layout was employed on a large scale. Although a variety of vegetables and grains are probably being cultivated, the images depict above all gardens with onions and leeks and enclosed orchards with rows of various palm trees, sycamores, figs, grapevines and pomegranate trees.

2400 BC: INSPIRATION I In the *Epic of Gilgamesh,* preserved on fragments of Babylonian tablets, the garden is described as a paradisiacal place, providing shade, water, fruit and pleasant fragrances for the desert dwellers.

CIRCA 2000 BC: HARD GARDEN WORK The record entitled *Life Lessons of the Cheti,* composed during the early 12th dynasty (Middle Kingdom), contains a vivid and detailed description of the rigours of gardening in the relentless sun: "The gardener carries the yoke; his shoulders are stooped with age. He has so many ulcers on his nape that it has the appearance of a festering wound. Of a morning, he waters the vegetables and in the evening the shade plants, and spends the entire day in the orchard. Then he falls over weary and tired, and for him this is true more than for any other trade." Under the strict rule of a supervisor, the gardener has to toil from morning to night. With the exception of the administrator and of course the owner, the workers are said to have sometimes even become victims of ridicule. Thus an image from Deir al-Medineh depicts a monkey watering flower beds from water jugs suspended from a yoke he carries across his shoulder. The tool for hauling water is a *shaduf,* a pole balanced on a beam and equipped with a water pail and a counterweight. Gardening tools such as hoes and sickles are also depicted on murals.

FROM 1600 BC: TOMB GARDENS I The tombs of wealthy Egyptians are embellished with tomb paintings. Opinions are divided on whether the images depict the real gardens of the owners or symbolic garden landscapes of religious significance. What is undisputed, however, is that garden design is also of religious importance and that plants are associated with the gods: thus, the date palm tree is associated with Re, the mulberry fig with Hathor and the tamarisk with Osiris. On the tomb painting of a scribe who had been in the employ of the granary, Hathor steps out from behind a tree, bearing provisions for the deceased.

CIRCA 1450 BC: IMPORT I The Egyptian Pharaoh Hatshepsut (circa 1490–1468 BC) initiates the import of foreign plants, a practice continued by her successor, Thutmose III (circa 1486–1425 BC). The oldest known "book of plants" is found in the wall reliefs at the Amun temple at Karnak in Egypt, handing down a record of the plants imported by Thutmose. Flowers are cultivated for bouquets, sacrificial

Garden work: mural from the tomb of Sennedjem showing a rectangular garden
with date and doum palms, sycamores and water channels.
From the ancient Egyptian city of Thebes, located on the Nile, ca. 1290 BC

rituals, embalming and medicinal purposes. The blue flowering water lily outshines all others as a sacred flower, as does the white flowering lotus. The latter is regarded as a symbol of rebirth because it dies in winter and grows again in spring. In early summer, the ponds in the temple and palace gardens are transformed into a blue-white carpet of blossoms.

1425 BC: TOMB GARDENS II A tomb painting depicts the walled garden at the Amun temple in Egypt. Lying adjacent to a canal, the garden has four ponds. The trees, plants and buildings are symmetrically arranged. This formal rhythm and the rectangular form would significantly influence all future garden plans, or conversely it seems to be a natural, practical and beautiful division and form for a garden then as now.

CIRCA 1000 BC: GAME PARKS The Assyrian King Tiglath-Pileser I (circa 1115–1077 BC) commissions the creation of vast game parks for hunting along the upper reaches of the Tigris. Undomesticated animals are kept there, but foreign plants are cultivated as well. These parks are considered to be the greatest treasure of the country and become a preferred target for destruction during armed conflicts. They are the early precursors of the medieval game parks and zoos, such as the *Royal Menagerie* in the Tower of London, which was built in 1235 under Henry III (1207–1272), which in turn prepared the ground for 19th-century landscape parks and the transformation of the latter into contemporary urban parks.

Similarly, in the area that is now China, the first game parks were laid out during that period, and they, too, mark the start of garden history in Asia. | 1859: CULTURAL TRANSFER VI, CHINOISERIE AND JAPONISM

FROM 850 BC: SACRED GROVE The Greek poet Homer described sacred gardens dedicated to the gods Apollo, Athena and Aphrodite – idyllic, sacred groves, meadows and creeks. The hot and arid climate that characterises Greece gives rise to myths about water sources and verdant, shaded settings: thus the nymph Calypso from the fifth book of Homer's epic poem *The Odyssey* dwells in a cave surrounded by poplars, cypresses, and alders: "A vine wound around the vaulted grotto, / Youthfully fresh, with vigorous foliage and heavy with grapes. / And four sources sprang forth there with scintillating water, / originating side by side and running here and there. / All around lush meadows flowered with violets and lark-spur. / Even an immortal, were he to travel this way, / Would gaze in amazement and feel joy in his heart." In this passage, Homer describes the prototype of the grottoes and nymphaeum follies that feature in the Baroque garden and the 19th-century landscape park.

However, with the exception of the utilitarian gardens near settlements, the sacred groves and the groups of black poplars, cypress and plane trees imported from northern Persia that are planted around gymnasia, temples and theatre complexes, there are no archaeological traces of gardens in Greece. Conversely, Greeks have cultivated potted plants since the Minoan era (3000–1200 BC) – probably bay trees, pomegranate trees and myrrh shrubs, and there are (tenure-) deeds that mention gardens. Greece's abundant flora is an aesthetic and botanical treasure trove: the some 6000 flowering plants and ferns provide healing plants as well as motifs for painting, ceramics and sculpture and would later enrich the gardens in northern Europe. The word "botany" is derived from "botane", which meant "grazing land for cattle" and "weed or herb" during Homer's time.

AFTER 750 BC: LANDSCAPE PARK I King Sargon II, Assyrian ruler from 722 to 704 BC, is one of the first to reconfigure a natural landscape: in Chorsabad in present-day northern Iraq, he shifts vast amounts of earth to alter the natural environment into an artificially designed landscape with man-made hills for vistas and terraced gardens. His son, King Sanherib (circa 741–681 BC), moves his residence and designs a garden on the banks of the Tigris to the northeast of Nineveh: this garden is supplied with water by means of a clever irrigation system comprising canals, so-called *qanats,* catch- and overflow basins and even by means of a 275-m-long aqueduct across a valley. This is a landscape park with cypresses, cedars, palm trees, cotton shrubs, vines, olive trees and winding paths for strolling at leisure.

24

Irrigation systems using *qanats* are still used today:
banana plantations on the island of Santiago, Cape Verde Islands

CIRCA 600 BC: THE GODDESS OF GARDEN DESIGN

The Greek poet Sappho (circa 612 to after 590 BC) describes a sacred grove of Aphrodite, dotted with apple trees and wild flowers and with a gurgling spring: "... Inside water, cool breeze through the apple branches and the roses everywhere lending shade, slumber falls gently from trembling leaves. (...) blossoming spring-coloured flowers, disperse honeyed scents in the winds." Aphrodite is the goddess of garden design associated with flowers; her son Eros is depicted as a gardener on a water vessel (hydria), which is now on display at the National Archaeological Museum of Athens.

AFTER 600 BC: HANGING GARDENS I

The Babylonian King Nebuchadnezzar II (605–562 BC) commissions the creation of the most famous terraced gardens, the *Hanging Gardens of Babylon,* for his wife Amytis, a Median princess pining for the green mountains of her homeland in the Sumerian capital of Babylon. They are also known as the *Hanging Gardens of Semiramis,* although the princess Semiramis is assumed to have lived in the 9th century BC. Centuries later, the gardens are still described as one of the seven wonders of the world. Excavations have failed to determine the exact location, but there are descriptions, for example those of the Chaldaic priest Berosus (circa 260 BC) and the historians Diodor of Sicily (circa 90–21 BC) and Strabo (63 BC to 28 AD): the terraces are supported by a walled-in, vaulted structure, 120 metres long on the sides. The terrace floors consist of a combination of cobblestones, rendered waterproof by means of a thin layer of tin. This base construction is covered in a layer of earth sufficiently deep to allow trees to root. Water is said to have been supplied via a tall pillar, continuously hollow from the bottom of the substructure to the very top, through which water from the Euphrates was drawn to the uppermost terraces with the help of a winch. From the top terrace, water was then distributed across the lower levels through an irrigation system. Palm trees, plum, cherry, pear, almond and apricot trees, wine, various climbing plants and flowers may have transformed this stepped structure into a kind of verdant mountain on which Amytis could go for walks and soothe her homesickness. Although the *Hanging Gardens of*

Wonder of the world: the legendary *Hanging Gardens of Babylon*. Coloured woodcut based on a drawing by Ferdinand Knab, 1886

Babylon are perhaps only a dream set into the world by poets and authors, those garden ensembles which the Babylonians did create demonstrate their mastery of transforming nature.

539 BC: CULTURAL TRANSFER I The Persians conquer Mesopotamia and adopt the garden culture of the Babylonians and Assyrians.

500–336 BC: PUBLIC PARKS I The Athenian politician Kimon (510–449 BC) has shade-giving plane trees planted on the agora of Athens and elm, poplars, olive and plane trees in the grove of the academy on the edge of the city. Cities like Athens are characterised by dense development, leaving little room for gardens and too little water. Even the courtyards are used as open-air workspaces – for cooking, laundry and keeping goats. On the edge of the city and in rural areas, there are utilitarian gardens where pumpkin, lettuce, onion, mint, myrrh, figs or fruit are grown. In addition, there is tremendous demand for flowers for cult rituals: wild flowers are gathered and roses, violets, myrtles, lilies and hyacinths are cultivated.

The potted gardens grown for the Feast of Adonis celebrated by women are called "Adonis gardens". For this, quickly sprouting seeds or seedlings are put in pots and placed on the rooftops; the plants then serve at the Adonis festival as a symbol of Adonis's rapid flourishing and early death. Without being watered, the plants wither again, which symbolises his death. Adonis, the symbol of beauty and vegetation, is Aphrodite's lover and when he is killed by Ares, the god of massacre and war, each of Aphrodite's tears turns into an adonis. The name refers to the scarlet red adonis flower rather than the yellow one; around thirty-five varieties are native to Europe and the cooler regions of Asia.

CIRCA 400 BC: PARADISE The Greek historian Xenophon (430 to circa 354 BC) describes the garden of Kyros the Great (601–530 BC) in Pasargadae in present-day Iran, which is now a Unesco World Heritage site. The garden is divided into four parts by watercourses and a pool at the centre, a symbolic translation of the idea of the four rivers of paradise and a recurring pattern in later Islamic gardens, then in medieval monastery gardens and until today in the cruciform paths bisecting many farmers' gardens. Under Kyros the Great, the water supply by means of *qanats* was further developed. Xenophon refers to the layout as "paradeisos". In Persia, the *paradeisoi* include not only paradisiac pleasure gardens, but also game parks and fruit plantations.

Aristotle (384–322 BC) also studies plants: nearly a century after Hippocrates' exploration of plants for medicine, his focus is on their nutritional qualities.

AFTER 400 BC: KITCHEN GARDENS Neither the central courtyard of the Greek home nor the atrium of the traditional Roman house is initially designed as a garden. Instead, the kitchen garden of the Romans lies behind the house, as revealed by excavations in the long-since abandoned town of Cosa in the Italian Maremma region.

334 BC: CULTURAL TRANSFER II The Macedonian King Alexander the Great (356–323 BC) conquers the Persian King Dareios III (circa 380–330 BC) and takes possession of his palaces at Babylon, Susa and Persepolis. His army also comes across large gardens, taking plants to the area of ancient Greece, where Aristotle and his disciple Theophrastes study them.

CIRCA 300 BC: PHILOSOPHERS' GARDENS Like Plato, Aristotle and Theophrastes, the Greek philosopher Epicure (341–270 BC) has a philosopher's garden where he cultivates vegetables among other plants with his own hands. His mind turns towards the earthly and the sphere of the senses. One should accept what nature has to offer with joy and also be content with it. This affirmation of conditions as they are, which also in the face of pain and perishability should not be abandoned, was possibly inspired by his work in the garden. In the meantime, the disciples of Plato and Aristotle are entered into the annals of history as "peripatetics", or "strollers", because they stroll along the paths that surround the academy and the lyceum, philosophising in the shade of the trees. Strolling through

Akademos-Park in Athens during discussion is meant to have a creative influence on one's thoughts. Theophrastes (372–287 BC), who has by now assumed the running of the philosophers' school in Athens as Aristotle's successor, creates the foundation for today's botany with his works *On the Origins of Plant Growth* and *A Natural History of Plants*. He describes some 450 legumes and herbs and other useful plants, flowers such as roses – incidentally, the word "rose" is derived from "Rhodes", where roses are cultivated – as well as carnations, marjoram, lilies, or peppermint.

AFTER 300 BC: TOMB GARDENS III The custom of surrounding graves with flowers spreads across Asia Minor and Egypt. In Alexandria, citizens can lease a tomb or graveyard lot outside the city walls for a period of five years to cultivate lettuce, cabbage, asparagus, leeks, melons, figs, grapes and dates – in others words, they are allowed to create allotments.

CIRCA 250 BC: FLOATING GARDEN I Hieron II (270–215 BC), also known as the Tyrant of Syracuse, is said to have created a lush garden on one of his ships: through hidden lead pipes it is watered; the plants grow in baskets filled with soil. Today there are *floating gardens,* for example on Inle Lake in Myanmar. People live in stilt houses and grow fruit and vegetables on the lake. They grow in a fertile mass of swampy soil which, held together by a meshwork of water hyacinths, is anchored to the bottom of the lake by bamboo poles. The gardens are cultivated by boat.

FROM 200 BC: PERISTYLE GARDEN AND ARCADIA I
On the arid island of Delos, villas are built around colonnaded courtyards in which rainwater is collected in basins. Sources differ as to whether they are planted and thus precursors to the Roman *peristyle gardens* or not. At any rate, the Roman *peristyle courtyard garden* becomes increasingly popular during the 2nd and 1st centuries BC. Although the Romans adopt Hellenistic and Egyptian influences, the idea of planting a garden in the colonnaded central courtyard, the peristyle, is undoubtedly their own.

Arcadia, the mountainous landscape of the Peloponnese in Greece, grows fallow through over-forestation and cultivation; in short, it is anything but a garden landscape. It is only in the 17th century – Nicolas Poussin's 1640–1645 painting *Et in Arcadia ego* marks a high point – that this landscape becomes the setting for a rural (shepherd's) lifestyle and synonymous with an idyllic landscape par excellence. The words "arcadia", "paradise" and "elysion", – in Greek mythology the "paradisiacal holy land" where eternal spring reigns – are often employed synonymously in the glorification of Antiquity during the 17th century. Swiss poet, painter and co-founder of the *Neue Zürcher Zeitung,* Salomon Gessner (1730–1788), for example, imagines in his *Idyllen* (1756) a country house in the shade of nut trees and a garden with fountains and beds where flavourful vegetables grow. It is a garden where he can relax far from the bemoaned hectic pace of the city. Gessner therewith formulates a desire that in the 20th century is realised so often in the form of a private home with garden that uncontrolled development of the landscape becomes a serious problem.

AD: BOTANY The Greek physician Pedanius Dioscorides (circa 40–90) from Anazarbos in today's Turkey composes the most important treatise of medicinal botany of Antiquity, the *Materia medica,* comprising some 500 plants. It is subsequently translated into Arabic and studied by botanists well into the 18th century. He is thus regarded as the trailblazer of the science of pharmacology.

60–65: GARDENING TIPS I The Roman nobleman Lucius Moderatus Columella (? – circa AD 70) writes a twelve-volume opus about creating a garden, about the irrigation, appropriate plants and their cultivation. He mentions the pruning of vines and hedges, the time when laurel, myrrh, and other evergreen plants should be seeded, frost protection methods by means of flat mats of woven reeds filled with straw and chaff, and discusses various fertilisers such as ash, charcoal and kitchen scraps. The work also includes descriptions of tools and tips on preventing the spread of diseases through mixed plantings or on how to fend off an ant infestation by planting heliotrope

Pharmacology: illustration for Pedanius Dioscorides' *Materia medica*.
Illuminated Islamic manuscript, 11th century

(vanilla flower). Many of these techniques are employed unchanged up to the end of the Middle Ages; and today they are being rediscovered in organic gardening and agriculture. Columella also reports that the Romans introduce flowers, spices and fruit – lilies and roses, then anise, dill, caraway, mustard and coriander as well as cherries, plums, peaches, apricots, almonds, walnuts and grapevines – into the area of present-day Germany.

AUGUST 79: POMPEII AND TOPIARY I Vesuvius erupts and buries Herculaneum, Pompeii and the villas in the environs of the cities beneath a thick layer of ash and lava. Pliny the Elder (23–79) perishes during the eruption. His *Historia naturalis,* a compendium on plants, animals, minerals and geography, mentions the Roman Gaius Matius (1st century BC), who invented the *opus topiari,* the art of pruning trees into a specific shape. The garden artist or *topiarius* uses scissors and sickles to trim cypress, ivy, box and yews into geo-metrical figures, animals, even hunting scenes and ships. This is the first time that plants are deliberately clipped into ornamental figures and employed as imaginary, sculptural and narrative motifs. A con-temporary example of a garden with extraordinary *topiaries* is the garden known as *Great Dixter* by Christopher Lloyd (1921–2006) in the south of England. Lloyd made a name for himself with numerous articles and especially with his book *The Well-Tempered Garden* (1970).

The eruption of Vesuvius, or rather the layers of lava, preserve the traces of life and the gardens in authentic form: in Pompeii gardens are part of public facilities such as schools, inns and temples, and also a standard feature of private homes. While larger villas may boast up to four *peristyle gardens,* even the simple house of a tradesman includes a courtyard garden. The Romans are without a doubt pas-sionate lovers of gardens. This is evident not only in their writings, it is also manifest in the urban planning, in their architecture and on murals. The walls of some courtyard gardens, for example, are embel-lished with perspectival murals that make this outdoor living space appear larger than it is. Columns and bowls, plants such as myrrh, ivy, oleander, roses, strawberries or lemon trees, birds and even mos-quitoes are depicted in the paintings. Nail holes in the walls suggest

Illusionistic painting: fresco featuring trees, flowers and birds, garden room of the Villa of Livia, Porta Prima, Italy, before 79

that fruit-bearing trees were likely trained along trellises and sculptures, works raided from the Greeks or copies of such pieces, were placed in the garden. The influence of Roman garden culture on the evolution of gardens in Europe and North America cannot be underestimated: the Romans bundle the history of gardens thus far into a synthesis of their own, advance irrigation techniques through aqueducts and water pipes and spread north of the Alps plants indigenous to the Mediterranean and Asia, as well as the art of raising trees from cuttings. | 1648: TREE NURSERY

97–107: VISTA Pliny the Younger (circa 61–115), nephew and heir of Pliny the Elder, writes letters on the theme of his two gardens in Tusculum and Laurentum in present-day Tuscany. He mentions how important the location and orientation of a garden are, specifying the wind and water conditions as well as exposure to the sun. His Villa Tusci has a garden in the shape of a hippodrome with fountains, round benches, vine-covered pergolas, a pleasure pavilion, rows of trees and beds bordered by box hedges. An ornamental garden, the *xystus,* lies in front of the villa's portico and the interior features a courtyard garden with plane trees and a fountain. He hints at the existence of greenhouses. An important element for future garden design is his description of the vista: from a height, the surrounding land, he says, appears "not like a real landscape, but like an exquisite painting".

118–138: NYMPHAEUM During his reign, the emperor Hadrian (76–138) builds a villa in Tivoli some 20 kilometres east of Rome. Ponds, columns, colonnaded halls, pavilions and statues are important elements of the gardens at the Villa Adriana, which has been declared a Unesco World Heritage site. The motifs of this Roman Garden would come to dominate the European history of gardens, thus the *nymphaeum,* known as the "Teatro Marittimo", a rotunda erected around a pond with an island at the centre.

269: VALENTINE'S DAY On 14 February, Bishop Valentine of Terni is executed upon an order issued by Roman Emperor Claudius II Gothicus (circa 214–270). According to legend, the Christian martyr

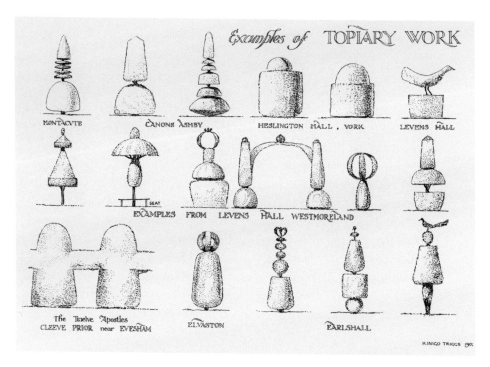

Examples of TOPIARY WORK

MONTACUTE   CANONS ASHBY   HESLINGTON HALL, YORK   LEVENS HALL

SEAT   EXAMPLES FROM LEVENS HALL WESTMORELAND

The Twelve Apostles
CLEEVE PRIOR near EVESHAM   ELVASTON   EARLSHALL

H.INIGO TRIGGS 190?

Animals and geometric figures: *topiary* designs,
engraving from 1902

Cones, cylinders, chess pieces: *topiary* in the *Victorian Garden* of Levens Hall, Kendal, Cumbria, England

A significant influence on the history of garden culture: the "Teatro Marittimo"
at the Villa Adriana in Tivoli, Italy

and subsequent saint used to give newlyweds flowers from his garden; marriages blessed by him seem to have been under an especially good star. From the 15ᵗʰ century onwards, Valentine couples are chosen in England and in 1667 the wife of the English diarist Samuel Pepys (1633–1703) is said to have responded to one of his love letters with a bouquet of flowers, a gesture that others begin to copy. English emigrants take the custom to the United States, and during the Second World War, it returns from there to Europe. But the custom only becomes popular and well known in the postwar era, thanks to the advertising campaigns of florists to present flowers on 14 February.

CIRCA 300: PATRONESS Saint Dorothea of Caesarea (circa 290 to circa 305) also dies a martyr's death during the persecution of Christians under Roman emperor Diocletian (244–311). According to legend, a boy takes a basket with roses and apples from Christ's heavenly garden to the court scribe Theophilus, as promised by Dorothea – and this although it is in the middle of winter. Dorothea becomes the patroness of gardeners and is depicted with a basket full of flowers and fruit.

CIRCA 500: GARDEN CARPET I Asia Minor is ruled by the Sassanids and the Byzantines, who engage in a veritable competition for the most extravagant garden. Emperor Constantine the Great (circa 280 to 337), who changes the name of the capital, Byzantium, to Constantinople in 330 (now Istanbul), and the Sassanid caliphs compete with gardens in which mechanically operated songbirds, fashioned from metal and gold, roaring lions and artificial trees are found. The Byzantine art of mosaics in churches and later in illuminated books is replete with garden motifs; ivy, roses, lilies, a variety of trees are depicted and animals cavort across the images. With the fall of the Roman Empire, Byzantium takes on the role of mediator between Eastern and Western (garden) culture. Constantine's palace, which serves as an official imperial residence for over 800 years, is destroyed by the Franks in the 13ᵗʰ century, and this is why nothing remains of his gardens.

The Sassanid King Chosroes I (531–579) for his part is said to have loved his garden more than the business of government. He commissions a garden carpet to be woven so that he may enjoy the view of flowers even in winter. According to legend, this garden carpet was more than 50 square metres large: the background of the carpet depicts the pleasure garden, trees and spring flowers. The border imitates flower beds, with the leaves and blossoms woven from silk, and gold woven into the stems and the yellowish earth, pearls, silver thread and crystal set into the gravel paths and water features. Many of these garden carpets – including smaller and far more modest ones – provide information on the design of gardens and plant species: in the form of a large cross, the garden is divided into four sections by four watercourses, with a fountain or basin marking the intersection of the latter. Pine trees, ash, elms, willow trees, cypress, maple, apricot, almond, cherry and lime trees, as well as swans, pelicans and numerous songbirds are depicted on these fairy-tale carpets. The idea of paradise as a garden is a source of inspiration for carpet motifs for centuries.

CIRCA 600: ISLAMIC GARDENS I AND CULTURAL TRANSFER III Mohammed, the founder of Islam, is born in this era (circa 570–632). Islam adopts existing ideas of the garden, elevates them onto the spiritual plane and translates the garden into an earthly paradise for believers: "Gardens with shade-giving branches, gardens in which sources flow, gardens in which there is a pair of each kind of fruit. There, believers rest comfortably on beds lined with brocade and the fruit in the gardens hang so low that one can easily pluck them." The Islamic culture with its rich ornamentation, calligraphy, architecture and science flourished gloriously, while Europe remained at a standstill after the collapse of the Roman Empire. Baghdad and later the Arabic-influenced city of Cordoba in Spain, become centres of science, art and the Oriental/Islamic garden culture. The first gardens are created in Cordoba, where fruit and flowers from the eastern Mediterranean, Persia and even India and China thrive. Garden ideas and plants travel from the Orient via Spain and Sicily to Europe, where they, in turn, enrich the palette of plant species and design

The idea of paradise as a garden is the source of inspiration for garden motifs.
At the same time tapestries witness the garden culture of their time: *Gartenbrunnen und Ententreiben*, ca. 1450/60 (detail)

Basic pattern of an Islamic garden with water channels:
Mughal School painting, 17ᵗʰ century, from the *Clive Album*,
Victoria & Albert Museum, London, England

in the Mediterranean and northern European regions. The Moors –
the Spanish name for Muslims – would have a lasting influence on
European garden culture with their knowledge. Both the gardens that
Spanish missionaries create in the arid Southwest of North America
in the 18th and 19th centuries and today's gardens in courtyards in
Andalusian homes are based on the same Islamic garden ideal. The
basic pattern of an Islamic garden, the *chahar bagh,* is once again
a division into four sections by means of water: "chahar" means "four",
"bagh" means "garden". A pond, sometimes a *chabutra,* a stone or
marble slab, or even a pavilion, mark the intersection. Water as the
source of life is staged and celebrated with great imagination, whereby the Arabs adopt the knowledge of building *qanats* from the Persians; the idea of employing colourful tiles to embellish water basins,
conversely, goes back to the ancient Egyptians.

These paradisiacal garden environments bring joy to body and
spirit and are simultaneously understood as *the* symbol of divine
creation: "Behold the upright posture of the Syrian rose and how
the violet genuflects (...). What I feel in all this is testimony of Your
Uniqueness, proof of Your Incomparability, that You are the All-
Presaging, the All-Knowing, the Only Truth."

CIRCA 800: GARDENING TIPS II Charlemagne (747–814)
releases the edict on the administration of crown lands, the *Capitulare de villis vel curtis imperii.* It contains tips on vegetable and
herb gardens and a list of recommended garden plants: these include
sage, hedge mustard, rosemary, lilies, roses, mallow, apples, pears,
quince, cherries, peaches, laurel and figs. Whereas some herbs such
as rosemary originate from the south but take well to being grown
in this region, other herbs such as wormwood and mugwort are
culled from the wild and grown in the garden. The garden culture
from Antiquity and the Arab world is adopted and perpetuated by
monasteries, where it is absorbed into Christian culture; monastery
gardens thus cast a bridge between the gardens of Antiquity and
those of the Renaissance.

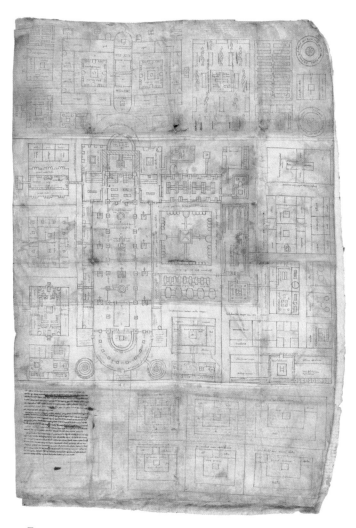

Europe's oldest garden plan: plan of the St. Gallen monastery
from 819, Switzerland

819: MONASTERY GARDEN I The garden plan of St. Gallen monastery in Switzerland is drafted. It is widely regarded as the oldest illustrated garden plan in Central Europe and is one of the most important sources for researching Carolingian garden culture. The monastery has been declared a Unesco World Heritage site. In addition to the vegetable garden (*hortus*), the herb garden (*herbularius*) and the orchard, which is identified as the monks' cemetery, there is a garden in the *cloisters* reminiscent of a Roman *peristyle garden*, as well as two "paradise" gardens. The term "paradise" in this context is reserved for areas directly adjoining the portals, which serve as meditative spaces and where roses – a symbol of the heavenly and the divine – are the dominant plant. At the centre of the crossing of paths in the *cloisters*, the plan envisions a juniper (*Juniperus sabina*). This represents a symbol with multiple meanings: on the one hand the juniper is known as a medicinal used for abortions (known in the vernacular as Mägdebaum or "maiden tree", *Jungfernpalme* or "virgin palm", savin tree), and on the other hand it is also a symbol of eternity and protection against evil spirits; the timber is used as incense. The plantings include onion, celery, parsnip, cabbage, sage, coriander, chervil, rosemary and mint, fennel and lovage, there are apple, pear and plum trees, medlar, laurel and quince and even sweet chestnut, fig and almond trees. All these plants and medicinal herbs are also listed in Charlemagne's *Capitulare de villis vel curtis imperii*. In addition to the herb and vegetable gardens, the plan also envisions spaces for spiritual renewal. The spatial programmes for Roman villa gardens and Oriental garden culture converge in this plan.

CIRCA 827: HORTUS CONCLUSUS I The German abbot and poet Walahfried Strabo (809–849) composes the poem *Liber de cultura hortorum,* usually referred to as *Hortulus,* in which he exhorts not only the creation and maintenance of a garden, but also the happiness and quality of life that a garden offers. The garden is a place of poetic transfiguration; despite the poetic form, however, the piece here also includes everyday tips on plants and cultivation methods. The Benedictine and poet, who serves as abbot at Reichenau monastery on Lake Constance from 839 onwards (today a Unesco

World Heritage site), has created one of the most important botanical works of the Middle Ages. Although reference is made to a "locus amoenus" or a "hortus deliciarum", a site for leisure and pleasure, the utilitarian garden takes precedence north of the Alps: the cultivation of plants serves to nourish people and livestock. The fact that the garden is surrounded by a wall and is thus a *hortus conclusus,* is founded in practical considerations – for example, to prevent livestock and wildlife from wandering into the garden – and corresponds to the medieval lifestyle: the environs of a village or town are not seen as a peaceful, uplifting landscape beckoning excursions as in Pliny's day, but instead a place where real (raids, wars) and supernatural (spirits, the powers of evil) dangers lurk.

CIRCA 1000: ISLAMIC GARDENS II Abd al-Rahman III (889–961), Caliph of Cordoba, has a vast palace and garden complex built from 929 onwards, the *Medina al-Zahra.* It serves as the seat of government until 1010, when the power of the caliph is overthrown by revolting Berbers and the palace is burnt to the ground.

The physician and botanist Ibn al-Wafid (circa 997–circa 1075) creates the palace garden *Huerta del Rey* in Toledo, Spain, which is said to have had a man-made lake in "whose centre stood a crystal pavilion; water was transported onto the roof, whence it fell down on all sides into the lake like artificial rain". After al-Wafid's death, his successor Ibn Bassal takes care of the garden, but is forced to flee to Seville when Toledo is re-captured by Christians in 1085. There he looks after the royal gardens and writes a book on agriculture which becomes the basis for other works authored by Arab experts on plants and gardens. When Seville is also conquered by Christians in 1248, all that remains is Granada, holding out as a small sultanate until 1492. Two of the most famous Islamic gardens in Europe that have survived to the present day are created here: the gardens of the Alhambra and of the Palacio de Generalife, both of which have in the meantime been declared Unesco World Heritage sites. | CIRCA 1319: 1001 ARABIAN NIGHTS I

Harmony of symmetry and water as mirror: in the garden of
the Alhambra, also known as Palacio de Comares or Myrrh Courtyard,
Granada, Spain

CIRCA 1147–1150: MONASTIC KNOWLEDGE The mystic, scientist, physician, philosopher and theologian Hildegard von Bingen (1098–1179) founds the Rupertsberg Monastery near Bingen on the Rhine. Her works *Causae et curae* (Causes and Cures), *Physica* and *Liber simplicis medicinae,* written at the monastery, are also milestones in the botanical knowledge of garden plants. Hildegard von Bingen describes some 200 plants, usually providing the German as well as the Latin name, and differentiates between healing and nutritional plants and ornamental plants. Even though her writings have no direct influence on garden design, the care with which she describes the plants once again elevates the knowledge of gardens, which has been pushed into the background in the wake of the collapse of the Roman Empire.

Yet medicinal plants are cultivated in addition to flowers and vegetables in many monasteries, thus at St. Gallen in Switzerland. Monks and nuns preserve the knowledge of the healing powers of plants; books on the medicinal properties of plants, such as the work entitled *Macer Floridus* written by the monk Odo Magdunensis (Odo de Meung-sur-Loire) most likely in the 11th century, and the manuscripts on herbs composed between the 12th and 15th centuries, the so-called *Circa instans* codices, are consulted as standard reference works. The library at the University of Basel, for example, houses a *Circa instans* on parchment containing some 380 illustrated entries on plants, and, less frequently, on animals and minerals. The texts and illustrations are part of a tradition that would later lead to the first printed German book on herbs, the *Gart der Gesundheit* (1485). Phyto-medicine is making a comeback today, although traditional knowledge on the effects of the plants is meanwhile supported by findings from clinical studies.

AFTER 1200: USE AND PLEASURE II Albertus Magnus (circa 1193–1280), a universally erudite man and the most important German theologian and philosopher of the Middle Ages, writes his opus *De vegetabilius, liber septimus de mutatione plantae ex silvestritate in domesticationem* around 1260 – a highlight in the history of gardens. It contains instructions on the design of a pleasure garden; the purpose of such a garden is relaxation. The trees offer shade, the meadow is ideal for strolling to and fro, pleasant aromas emanate from the "spice garden" as Magnus writes, which also lifts the spirits through a show of colour and the centre is occupied by a fountain, the symbol of the source of life. Plant-covered *lawn benches* are en vogue: they are box-shaped elevations that provide a place to sit and chat. The garden is a refuge for an elevated and carefree mode of living and – as in Islam – an expression of divine creation. Magnus also recommends the cultivation of grapes, fruit and spices such as saffron, parsley, coriander or lovage as well as peonies, lilies or marigolds; he prefers box as an ornamental shrub.

CIRCA 1225–1280: INSPIRATION II AND THE MEDIEVAL LOVE GARDEN Guillaume de Lorris (circa 1205–after 1240) writes his highly successful *Roman de la Rose,* composed of more than 22000 quatrains, which is completed from verse 4,059 onwards by Jean de Meung (circa 1240–circa 1305) in France. The protagonist, Amant, steps into a garden outside the city gates, which is rendered in great detail and becomes the setting for an allegorical play of love: encounters with allegorical figures are described in the form of a dream. Amant falls in love with a rose. Lovers in the garden and allegorical love gardens are also a popular motif in woodcuts and paintings; the garden of paradise has become a pleasure garden, it is a symbol of both heavenly and earthly love. Morally, the connection between the garden and eroticism is associated both with a positive and a negative connotation: positive in the sense of *The Little Garden of Paradise,* as the Upper Rhenish Master painted it circa 1410/1420, and negative in the sense of lack of chastity. | 1410 TO 1420: HORTUS CONCLUSUS II

In Europe, the garden has become not only a fixture of courtly aristocratic and monastic life, but also of urban and rural everyday life. While fortresses and castles feature pleasure gardens as well – the ideal of the *medieval love garden* by far survives the society of knights and medieval lyrics – the peasant garden, which is divided into four beds by two paths, provides chiefly a crop of vegetables, berries and fruit, as well as medicinal herbs and spices in addition to

Garden dance: illustration from the verse novel *Le Roman de la Rose*, ca. 1460.
Illumination for the Jouvenel des Ursins family, between 1447 and 1460,
possibly by Jean Fouquet (ca. 1420 to 1480)

flowers. Townspeople cultivate vegetable gardens for their own supply that run along the length of the city wall or between the ditches and ramparts of the suburb (in the *suburbium*). Peonies and monkshood are grown as both ornamental and medicinal plants.

CIRCA 1305: LOVE OF GEOMETRY I The Italian jurist Pietro de' Crescenzi (1233–1320/21) writes his book *Opus ruralium commodorum*. Based on Antique Roman texts, his own observations and the knowledge gained by Dominican monks at the monastery in Bologna, the book offers practical advice and influences the development of garden design with the idea of creating beds in geometrical forms.

CIRCA 1319: 1001 ARABIAN NIGHTS I In Spanish Granada, the upper garden of the Palacio de Generalife is created, followed some time later by the myrrh courtyard of the Alhambra. Cooled by the snow-capped Sierra Nevada, the gardens lie sheltered behind walls; the architecture of the buildings – embellished with artful stalactite vaults in stucco, faceted details, open-work honeycomb and arabesque patterns, colonnades, pavilions and pools – are perhaps the last instance of bringing a splendid palace garden in the style of the *1001 Arabian Nights* to life on European soil.

1348: INSPIRATION III The Italian poet Giovanni Boccaccio (1313–1375) begins to write *Il Decamerone*. At the centre of the collection of novellas is a group of young people who have fled to the countryside just outside Florence to escape the plague. To distract themselves from the horrors of the Black Death, they tell 100 unusually realistic, witty and titillating tales. Boccaccio not only describes a wealth of flowers and fruits, he also praises the design, the plan of the gardens, which he considers the quintessence of a cultivated landscape. In a number of the stories appear gardens that are meant to have been inspired by the garden of the Villa Palmieri in Florence, which was completely transformed to a Baroque garden in 1697 and expanded in the 19th century.

Working in geometrically laid-out beds:
illumination from Pietro de' Crescenzi's book *Opus ruralium commodorum*,
between 1475 and 1500

CIRCA 1410–1420: HORTUS CONCLUSUS II An unknown artist, called the Upper Rhenish Master, paints *The Little Garden of Paradise*. Mary is shown in a *hortus conclusus*, a garden surrounded by a wall; lilies of the valley, peonies, irises, white lilies and strawberries grow here, as well as other plants. The motif of the enclosed flower garden originates from the *Song of Solomon* and is very popular as a symbol for Mary's immaculate conception: "A garden locked is my sister, my bride, / A rock garden locked, a spring sealed up. (…) My beloved has gone down to his garden, / To the beds of balsam, / To pasture his flock in the gardens / And gather lilies." The *hortus conclusus* is chosen as a frequent setting depicted in prayer books and books of hours, first seen in those painted by the Limbourg brothers and then in the *Très riches heures* painted by Jean Colombe (circa 1430–circa 1493) for the Duc du Berry (1410–1485) or in Martin Schongauer's (1445/1450–1491) *Madonna im Rosenhag* (1473). | 1554: FLOWER LANGUAGE

CIRCA 1450: ANTIQUITY REDISCOVERED I The humanists of the Renaissance set in motion a first rediscovery of Antiquity. New ideas on human dignity and the living conditions required for it, which are founded in an education based on the literature, philosophy and science of Antiquity, also change attitudes towards nature and garden design: once again, the garden becomes a place for living *en plein air*, for conviviality and philosophical discourse. In his ten-volume opus on architecture *De re aedificatoria*, Leon Battista Alberti (1404–1472), Italian humanist and architect, describes Antique villas and gardens, thereby furnishing the basis for the European Renaissance garden.

1453: TULIPS AND LILIES The Ottoman sultans conquer Byzantium. The more powerful the Ottomans become – in the 18th century they reach the gates of Vienna – the greater is the flow of plants, bulbs and seeds that reaches Central Europe via Constantinople; carnations, hyacinths, tulips, narcissi, lilies and roses are especially popular.

The garden is an enclosed property, a *hortus conclusus*,
and each plant has its symbolic meaning: *The Littel Garden of Paradise*
Upper Rhenish Master, ca. 1410/1420

1483: USE AND PLEASURE III Kaspar von Effinger (1442–1513) purchased the Wildegg Castle in Switzerland, which had been built in the 12th century by the counts of Habsburg. The ensemble, comprising castle and kitchen, pleasure and rose gardens as well as an aviary, vineyard, forest and farm, is currently preserved in near original state. Until 1912, when Julia von Effinger (1837–1912), who resided as the eleventh generation on the estate, died without any heirs, the garden was a supplier of vegetables and fruit, as well as a recreation site. The Baroque garden is currently unique in Switzerland: flourishing on a terrace in the midst of the vineyard are around 300 old cultivated plants that are cared for in collaboration with the Pro Specie Rara foundation.

1494: CULTURAL TRANSFER IV The French King Charles VIII (1470–1498) moves on Naples at the head of an army to enforce the claim to power of the House of Anjou. Although his campaign fails, upon his return to Château d'Amboise on the Loire River he writes to the Duke of Bourbon: "My brother, you cannot imagine what beautiful gardens I have seen in this city. Truthfully. It seems that only Adam and Eve were lacking to transform them into paradise on earth, so beautiful and full of great and wonderful things are they." As a result Château d'Amboise would see the creation of a Renaissance garden in the Italian vein – the cultural transfer from Italy to France and the other European countries runs its course – and Louis XII, Charles's successor and equally passionate garden enthusiast, imports marble fountains from Italy. Jacques Androuet du Cerceau's (1510–1584) etchings are likely faithful reproductions of the original design of the gardens at Amboise, Châteaux de Gaillon and Blois, even though they are created much later, around 1607.

1499: INSPIRATION IV AND WATER GARDENS Francesco Colonna's (1433/34–1527) *Hypnerotomachia Poliphili* is published in Venice. The allegorical novel and the woodcuts that accompany it have a tremendous influence on garden design. The French King François I (1494–1547) is among those who are captivated by the tree- and flower-bed shapes described in it and commissions his garden

The beauty of water: garden of Château de Fontainebleau;
the name is derived from "fontaine belle eau", Seine-et-Marne, France

at Fontainebleau to be designed after this model from 1528 onwards; the ensemble has been declared a Unesco World Heritage site. An abbreviated French translation is published in 1546, followed in 1547 by an English translation. The arts and garden culture of the Renaissance flourish under François I in France. Among other projects, he initiates the creation of an ornamental garden with four sections of *flower beds* at Fontainebleau, with an Antique statue of Diana at the intersection of the axes (today housed in the Louvre). Under Caterina de' Medici (1519–1589), it is renamed *Jardin de la Reine.* The *Cour de la Fontaine,* a courtyard with fountain that borders a man-made lake, can be found in the part that is now called *Galerie François-1er*. Water plays an essential role at Fontainebleau from the outset. Over the ensuing years, water plays with sometimes highly complex hydraulic drives are built in many European gardens. The Baroque garden later features canals, pools and theatrical fountains with groups of figures as an important structuring principle.

PRE-1500: GARDEN CARPET II The Gobelins cycle dedicated to the five senses of sight, hearing, scent, touch and taste – *Les tapisseries de la dame à la licorne* – is created in France. In the tradition of garden-themed rugs, it features the Virgin and the legendary unicorn surrounded by flowers, trees, dogs, hares, monkeys and lions.

CIRCA 1500: ARTIFICIAL MOUNTAIN I The English King Henry VIII (1491–1547), who perceives his position to be one of cultural rivalry with François I, commissions the creation of the first significant English Renaissance gardens at his country residences of Hampton Court, Palace of Whitehall and Nonsuch Palace, which are also characterised by Italian influences. The park at Hampton Court (London) features a *montagnette* – a small man-made mount – from which the King can have an overview of the castle and the garden. Today, it is the site of the annual Hampton Court Flower Show, the largest garden and flower show in the world apart from London's Chelsea Flower Show and the Tatton Park Flower Show near Manchester. | 1804 AND 1851: GARDEN EXHIBITION I AND II The English begin to embrace the Roman and Greek (garden) culture with enthusiasm,

De groene Parnaßus-Berg Nº 8.

Perspective: artificial mountain, also known as *Parnassus, Gazebo* or *Montagnette*.
Engraving by Johannes van den Aveele, ca. 1700

Sunken parterre garden: the *Sunken Garden* at Pierrepont House in Nottingham, England. Painting by an unknown master, ca. 1705

developing a new awareness of landscape and how to design it. The *Sunken Garden* emerges as a unique feature of the English Renaissance garden: this is a *parterre garden* lowered into the ground, an example of which is found at Hanbury Hall in Worcestershire. In 1996, Dominique Perrault (*1953) creates a modern *Sunken Garden* with his design for the garden courtyard at the Bibliothèque Nationale de France in Paris.

Sebastiano Serlio (1475–1554), Italian architect and architecture theoretician, designs symmetrical, axial node and spiral patterns and concentrically arranged ornamental circles and rectangles which dominate the design of *parterre beds* throughout the Baroque and beyond. | FROM 1600: GARDEN PARTERRE

1530: MOGUL GARDENS The descendant of Genghis Khan (1162–1227) and founder of the Indian Mogul dynasty, Babur (also Babar, Baber; 1483–1530), dies in Agra, India. The dynastic ruler, who writes poetry, plays instruments and has a love of plants, leaves behind a legacy of gardens in Afghanistan's Kabul and Pakistan's Lahore. He collects tulips and writes movingly about the atmosphere and moods in his gardens. Deeply impressed by the gardens of his predecessor Timur-Leng (1336–1405), which he had seen in Samarkand, the *Bagh-e Babur* or Gardens of Babur, are said to have been modelled on the design of the former. He imports plants from Afghanistan to India and dispatches mangoes, cooking bananas, banyan trees and oranges to Kabul. His son, his nephew and the nephew's sons distinguish themselves in the years that follow with the creation of magnificent temple, palace and garden ensembles: highlights are the *Shalamar Gardens* in Lahore, created by Shah Jahan in 1642, and the Taj Mahal in Agra, a mausoleum erected from 1632 to 1654 for his wife Mumtaz Mahal (1593–1631) in an 18-hectare park, both of which have been declared Unesco World Heritage sites. The *Bagh-e Babur* in Kabul, a popular *Mogul terraced garden* for the inhabitants of Kabul, is destroyed after 1992 as a result of the war and the nearly complete deforestation. From 2000, the Aga Khan Trust for Culture, among others, has supported the restoration, and the park has been on the list of candidates to become a Unesco World Heritage site since 2009.

Place of contemplation in the metropolis:
Peter Zumthor's Serpentine Gallery Pavilion, London 2011. The garden design for
this *hortus conclusus* is by the Dutch garden designer Piet Oudolf.

1536: PUBLIC PARKS II The English King Henry VIII has the grounds around his Hyde estate fenced in so that he can hunt there; this would later become London's *Hyde Park*. Under King James I (1566–1625) the nobility has access to it, and from 1637 it is open for the city's residents. Under Queen Caroline of Ansbach (1683–1737), *Hyde Park* and *Kensington Gardens* are redesigned as a coherent landscape by Charles Bridgeman (1690–1738), which is completed in 1733. Bridgeman also lays out the curvy lake, *The Serpentine,* by damming the Westbourne and Tyburn rivers. The Serpentine Bridge, built by John Rennie (1794–1874) in 1826, separates the lake into The Long Water and the Serpentine River; since 1830 the lake has been fed by water from the Thames. In 1851, the park is the venue for the Great Exhibition and location of the *Crystal Palace.* | 1851: GARDEN EXHIBIT II A pavilion created by architects and artists is built near the Serpentine Gallery every summer: in 2011 it was a pavilion by Swiss architect Peter Zumthor (*1943) entitled *Garden Within a Garden;* the beds were designed by the Dutch garden designer Piet Oudolf (*1944), who also collaborated on the *High Line Park* in New York City and designed the garden grounds around the exhibition halls of the Galerie Hauser & Wirth in the English county of Somerset. Gardens and parks always bear the mark of their era. Over time, they also constitute a site's unmistakable character and generate identity among those who live there.

FROM 1542: MONSTER GARDEN Count Vicino Orsini (1523–1585) begins to lay out the garden at the Villa Orsini, the *Sacro Bosco* in Bomarzo, Italy. This is a labyrinthine, Mannerist fantasy garden replete with water features, allegorical figures, droll monsters, dragons and animals – for example, a turtle and an elephant hewn from a rock. There are also numerous literary allusions, encoded inscriptions and a crooked house. All these elements combine in the garden to confuse the sense of usual perception, promoting a feeling of wonder and amazement among visitors.

1545: SCIENCE I The *Orto Botanico di Padova* is established: it is a *hortus medicus,* a garden of healing herbs that is today a Unesco World Heritage site. Botanical gardens are founded in conjunction

Called a "Living Library": the *Botanic Garden*
founded in 1632 in Oxford, England

Grotto with the marble statue *La Schiava* by the Italian sculptor Antonio Canova (1757–1822)
and the *Fountain of the Dragon* in the *Giardini Botanici Hanbury*,
La Mortola near Ventimiglia, Italy.
Papyrus thrives in the protected climate around the fountain.

with the foundation of universities and are initially reserved for the cultivation of healing plants and the training of doctors; it is only later that rare or exotic (ornamental) plants and the idea of public education become integrated into the concept. After Padua, Pisa (1547), Bologna (1567), Leipzig (circa 1580), Cologne and Wroclaw (1587) and Oxford (1632) all see the emergence of botanical gardens. In 1577, the botanist Carolus Clusius (1526–1609) from the Netherlands founds the botanical garden of the University of Leiden. He travels through Europe, publishes books on the Spanish (1576) and Austrian (1583) flora, explores the alpine flora, introduces the potato and the chestnut to Austria and cultivates tulips, hyacinths, irises and gladioli. Europe is in the grip of tulip mania. Particularly beautiful examples today are also the *Giardini Botanici Hanbury* in La Mortola on the Italian Riviera, which have been the property of the University of Genoa since 1987. The English businessman Thomas Hanbury (1832–1907), who earned a fortune in Shanghai trading in spices, tea and silk, purchased the roughly 18-hectare plot sloping down to the sea in 1867 and employed, among others, the German garden designer Ludwig Winter (1846–1912). Over time, a garden was created with plants from around the world – also thanks to Hanbury's brother Daniel, who imported plants. Already by 1889, around 3,600 species are listed. Along with the olives, citrus fruit and cypresses native to the Mediterranean are the *Japanese Garden,* the *Scented Garden,* the *Australian Forest,* Brazilian guavas, collections of succulents and roses, and around 325 types of aloe, wisteria, passionflower and hibiscus. The garden has been a Unesco World Heritage site since 2006.

1546: THE GARDEN AS STAGE The garden and the Château de Chenonceau, erected by the French King Henri II (1519–1559) between 1551 and 1555 for his mistress Diane de Poitiers (circa 1500–1566) and passing into the hands of Caterina de' Medici from 1560 onwards, is a water castle par excellence with a Renaissance garden equally magnificent as that at Saint-Germain-en-Laye, leading down to the Seine via six terraces and having the appearance of a stage set: stage design, painting and garden art would be characterised by interdisciplinary inspiration in the years that followed. In contrast

Water castle with Renaissance garden and large forest: the Château de Chenonceau built on and over the River Cher is among the most beautiful castles in the Loire Valley, Indre-et-Loire, France.

to many French Renaissance gardens, which became dilapidated over time or were transformed into Baroque gardens and then into English landscape parks, the garden at Château de Villandry near Tours is once again a Renaissance garden today: this is thanks to the efforts of the Spanish physician Joachim Carvallo (1869–1936), who purchased the castle in 1906 and had the Baroque elements removed and the Renaissance garden reconstructed. To Carvallo, the Lost Paradise is a "garden of intelligence", not of sentiment. His dedicated study of sources notwithstanding, the reconstruction is also a new interpretation. One highlight is the so-called *potager*, a vast vegetable garden: in spring, the box-hedge-bordered beds are seeded with some 60 000 vegetables and flowers, followed by another 30 000 in summer. The sequence of harvesting and flowering requires a different garden plan each year, whereby all the plants are arranged in so dense and artful a manner as to form an ornament that is reminiscent of inlay work. In autumn, the ornamental cabbage shines in colours ranging from white to violet. The geometrically arranged beds, dispersed across nine square compartments, are reached via cruciform paths and even the tall rose trees are intended as reminders of medieval monastery gardens. At Château de Prangins, built in the 1730s high above Lake Geneva, is another *potager* that is worth a visit. The castle has housed part of the Swiss National Museum's collection since 1998.

1554: FLOWER LANGUAGE The tapestry *The Annunciation in Hortus Conclusus* (1554) was woven – probably in Zurich – from wool, linen, silk, metal threads and human hair; it depicts Mary's Immaculate Conception. Preserved today in the Benedictine Collegium Sarnen in central Switzerland, the devotional carpet shows in a rare, well-preserved beauty, Mary sitting in a walled garden waiting for the archangel Gabriel. He has four dogs with him, which stand for the virtues: truth, peace, justice and mercy. Mary touches the horn of a unicorn and is surrounded by numerous naturalistically depicted animals and plants. The iris represents altruism, the lily chastity, the rose symbolises Mary, but also stands for love, virginity, discretion and humility. Fruit trees refer to resurrection, strawberries to purity,

Nutrition and pleasure: the *potager* – the vegetable or kitchen garden –
in the Botanic Garden, Oxford, England

Potager in the Botanic Garden Oxford, England

Mary in the garden: *The Anunciation in Hortus Conclusus,* 1.55 × 4.21-metre tapestry
woven from wool, linen, silk, metal threads and human hair.
Produced in 1554 probably in Zurich,
preserved today in the Benedictine Collegium Sarnen, Switzerland.

Christ's spilled blood, and at the same time, to seduction! Lilies of the valley stand for chaste love and medicine, primroses for hope and innocence, jonquils for eternal life and fertility and daisies for power and faithfulness.

1560: RENAISSANCE Upon a commission from Cardinal Ippolito II d'Este (1509–1572), work begins on the construction of the Villa d'Este in Tivoli and the adjacent gardens; the design is created by the painter, architect and archaeologist Pirro Ligorio (1513–1583) and realised by the court architect Alberto Galvani. Construction and conversion works on the complex, which has since been declared a Unesco World Heritage site, continue until the end of the 17th century. In the 18th century, the garden falls increasingly into disrepair and is only saved from complete decay from the mid-19th century by Gustav Adolf, Cardinal Prince of Hohenlohe-Schillingsfürst (1823–1896). The garden consists of the hanging garden with its sequence of ramps, steps and terraces and the flat *Giardino delle Semplici* with flower beds and covered walks. Below the hanging garden, three fish ponds are arranged in succession in the transverse axis terminating in a double terrace with the imposing Neptune Fountain, also called water-organ, which Franz Liszt (1811–1886) is said to have played. Between 1867 and 1882 the composer was a frequent guest at the villa where he created *Giochi d'acqua*. In addition to these fountains, the *Avenue of the Hundred Fountains,* the *Tivoli Fountain* in the hanging gardens and the *Fontana di Roma* (largely demolished in 1855) gain world renown. The various areas of the garden act like rooms where one can sojourn and where fabulous parties take place.

Near the ruins of Tusculum, in Frascati and environs, a series of luxurious villas with Baroque gardens are built between 1550 and 1650, for example the Villa Aldobrandini (circa 1600) with its vast park in which small plane tree forests, spectacular waterworks and mythological figures seem to form a Mediterranean anteroom to paradise.

1563: LOVE OF GEOMETRY II AND AMPHITHEATRE I
Bernard Palissy (circa 1510–1590), French painter, ceramicist and glass artist, shares his vision of a Renaissance garden in his work *Recepte*

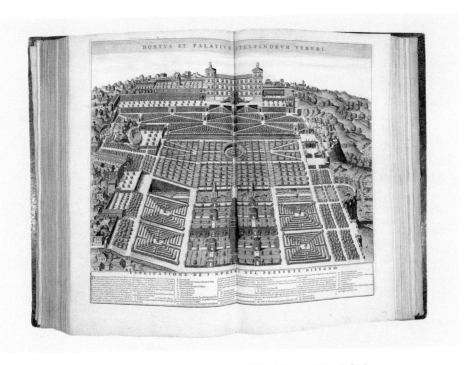

Open-air chamber: garden of the Villa d'Este in Tivoli, Italy.
Engraving by the cartographer and copperplate engraver Joan Blaeu (1596–1673)
from the book *Theatrum Civitatum*, 1663

véritable (1563): divided by avenues into four equal sections, the centre accommodates an amphitheatre, while the corners feature grottoes; the avenues debouch into small cabinets in the form of Antique temples. Palissy's compatriot, Charles Estienne (1504–1564), successful publisher and physician, explores the theme of practical garden design and work in his book *L'agriculture et maison rustique* (1583): he distinguishes between kitchen garden, flower and pleasure garden, as well as orchards, and describes arrangements for a variety of plants. The German priest Johann Peschel (circa 1535–1599) goes into even greater detail in his treatise on garden design published in Eisleben in 1597. Like Estienne, Peschel is a proponent of geometrical patterns. Trellises, labyrinths composed of man-high hedges and trees planted in the *quincunx ornament* – in which trees are arranged to form straight lines regardless from which angle they are seen – demonstrate his love of order: "For order is always lovely to behold."

CIRCA 1600: GROTTOES AND FOUNTAINS AND AMPHITHEATRE II

The Italian painter of Flemish origin, Giusto Utens (?–1609), paints fourteen villas and their gardens for the ceiling vaults at the ballroom of the Villa La Ferdinanda on commission by Ferdinand I de' Medici (1549–1609). Painted from a bird's-eye perspective, the images depict Tuscan villa gardens from the mid-14th century onwards. Standard elements in a ducal Renaissance garden are *flower beds,* fountains, pools with rocks and figures, grottoes, labyrinths or small mounts – called *montagnettes.* The garden of the Medici Villa di Pratolino north of Florence is one of the most impressive: planned as a spacious refuge for the prince and his lover, has several grottoes in the garden with mechanically operated figures – for example, ducks sipping water and a strolling virgin – a *montagnette* in whose centre a water-organ played, and a theatre for the amusement and entertainment of those taking a stroll.

The gardens of the Cortile del Belvedere in the Vatican, the Villa d'Este in Tivoli or the already somewhat Baroque garden of the Villa Lante in the Bagnaia quarter in Viterbo are stunning examples of Italian Renaissance gardens. The transition towards the Baroque is gradual: although the *Giardino di Boboli* in Florence originates in

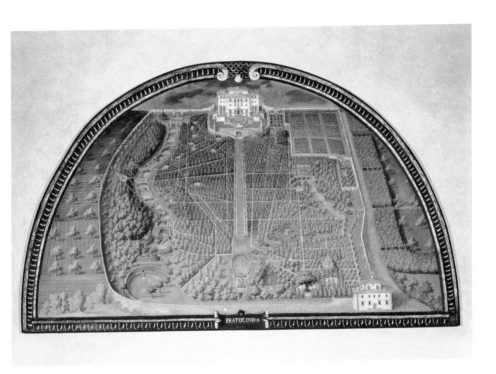

Bird's-eye view: *Villa di Pratolino*, lunette by Giusto Utens, 1599.
The park of the Medici Villa di Pratolino in Vaglia, Italy, has been owned
by the City of Florence since 1981.

the Renaissance, it is widely regarded as an important exponent of Baroque gardens. In 1549, the landscape architect Niccolò Tribolo (circa 1500–1550) transforms the small valley that lies behind the Palazzo Pitti into an amphitheatre and bisects the ensemble with a central avenue. Similar to Tribolo's design for the Villa Medici in Castello, the slopes are structured by various green garden spaces, *Giardino di Boboli,* subsequently complemented by architectural elements. The dolphin-shell fountain and the ocean fountain are part of a clever irrigation system, and groups of sculptures and numerous potted plants create variety in the lush garden.

FROM 1600: MAZE The Frenchman Olivier de Serres (1539– 1619) compares the process of the design of a *garden parterre* with the creative activity of a painter and differentiates between *compartments, quarters* and *parterres:* a *compartment* is a larger bed with ornamental plantings, several *compartments* together form a *quarter* *(quarreau),* and the joining of several quarters, in turn, creates a *parterre.* De Serres favours box as borders for beds, because it can also be shaped into *topiaries* – pyramids, columns and animals. He visits the gardens of Fontainebleau, Saint-Germain-en-Laye, Blois, the *Jardin des Tuileries* and the *Jardin du Luxembourg,* to report on the layout and ornamentation of the beds.

Hedge mazes and labyrinths gain in popularity; the labyrinths at Chatsworth in Derbyshire, Hampton Court, and *Glendurgan Garden* in Cornwall, England, | 1820: THE GRACES OF WILDERNESS II and the labyrinth at the Villa d'Este and in the cloister of the Monasterio de San Lorenzo in Santiago de Compostela, Spain, gain widespread fame.

1610: GARDEN PARTERRE The French King Henri IV is murdered in this year. His widow, Maria de' Medici (1575–1642), flees the Louvre and crosses the Seine where she purchases land from François de Luxembourg on which she builds a castle and the *Jardin du Luxembourg.* The *Giardino di Boboli* in Florence begun in 1549, serves as a model; however, because the site cannot be transformed into terraces, the only "Tuscan aspect" is the large avenue that runs crosswise instead of aligned with the central axis of the castle.

Bewildering geometry: labyrinth in the *Herrenhauser Gardens,* Hanover, Germany, laid out in 1937 based on a plan from 1674. The design is thought to have been originated by the French Baroque gardener Henri Pérronet (?–1690), who worked in Germany.

Water for the King's fountains: the *Machine de Marly*,
with which water from the Seine was pumped into the park of Versailles.
Painting by Pierre-Denis Martin (1663–1742) from 1722

Jacques Boyceau de la Barauderie (1560–1633), garden artist in the employ of Henri IV and Louis XIII, designs a *parterre* in 1612 in which the box ornaments are based on the motif of the acanthus leaf.

1613: BAROQUE André Le Nôtre (1613–1700) is born in Paris as the son of a famous family of gardeners. His father is in charge of the *Jardin des Tuileries,* a task that Le Nôtre would later assume. To begin with, however, he studies painting and architecture and then turns to garden design, which is regarded as equal to the fine arts for the first time. His first independent commission for a garden is to create the ensemble at Vaux-le-Vicomte near Melun, which is realised at tremendous expense in personnel and cost and for which three villages are said to have been razed to the ground. These gardens, which are inaugurated in 1661 with much pomp and ceremony, establish his fame and earn him the task, in 1662, of designing the park at Versailles of Louis XIV. An inhospitable swamp is transformed into a breath-taking garden ensemble, the symmetrical axes of which radiate all the way to the horizon, and whose *parterres* and *boskets* – small pleasure forests in geometrically designed Baroque gardens – garden rooms, sculptures, fountains and the reflecting Grand Canal are emulated throughout Europe and Russia. The ensemble is now a Unesco World Heritage site. In 1684, the *Machine de Marly* is constructed as an enormous pump station for the fountains, drawing water from the Seine across an aqueduct to the fountains, although the pressure is too low to operate all fountains simultaneously. Therefore, the *fontainier* conducts the water in such a manner that only those fountains within the King's view are running at any given time. Le Nôtre's gardens epitomise the art of the Baroque garden and are a symbol of absolutist power politics: those who follow this path, will at some point be led to the centre. He also designs parks for the castles at Trianon, Saint-Cloud, Marly-le-Roi, Meudon and Fontainebleau. The clarity in plan, the dramatic treatment of perspectives and the abundant variety make them spectacular settings for garden parties. Louis XIV personally wrote the garden guide *La manière de montrer les jardins de Versailles* between 1689 and 1705 in six versions, in which the places of interest are compiled as a tour. In addition, he has the hunting pavilion in the park developed into a small zoo with enclosures. And *topiary* – the art of trimming trees into shapes – reaches its apotheosis. Spheres, pyramids, cubes, columns and complex combinations of these shapes embellish the gardens at Versailles. Louis XIV is even said to have appeared at a costume ball disguised as a *topiary* tree.

Hunting lodges are being surrounded by a star-shaped system of paths, the *Étoile*, whereby the avenues or hedge-lined paths radiate out from the castle, potentially into infinity. Although the clear layout of the paths serves for hunts with horses and dogs, it also corresponds to the precept with a centre that governs the era of absolutism. This form of design with axes or *étoiles* and a secondary circle of buildings continues to be popular until the end of the 18th century.

1620: CULTURAL TRANSFER V Inspired by extensive travels in Italy, Sebastiano Serlio's *parterre* designs and Francesco Colonna's *Hypnerotomachia* (1499 published in Italy), the French garden artist and engineer Salomon de Caus (1576–1626) designs a vast garden complex in Heidelberg, Germany – the *Hortus Palatinus*. In addition to the *Leonberger Pomeranzengarten,* created circa 1611 by Heinrich Schickhardt (1558–1635), the *Hortus Palatinus* also decisively influences the evolution of German Baroque gardens. All that remains today is a copy of the sculpture *Vater Rhein* and an oil painting by Jacques Fouquières (1580–1659) depicting the garden. Through his travels and commissions in Belgium and England, de Caus also serves as a mediator of Italian garden art. Soon, German and Austrian members of aristocratic or bourgeois families begin to incorporate garden culture into the humanist education as part of their "Grand Tour" through Italy and to create Italianate gardens north of the Alps. Two gardens in particular are likely to have served as models: the Baroque garden at the Villa Garzoni in Collodi, created 1633–92, and the garden on Isola Bella on Lago Maggiore, where the Count Carlo Borromeo and his sons transformed an entire island into a ship-like palace with terraced gardens from 1632 onwards.

Epitome of Baroque garden art: *Vue du château de Versailles en 1668*, painting by the French landscape painter Pierre Patel (1605–1676)

Floating garden: *Isola Bella, Lago Maggiore* (1819),
painting by the Swiss painter Mathias Gabriel Lory (1784–1846)

1625: COMPOSED WILDERNESS The English philosopher and statesman Francis Bacon (1561–1626) publishes his essay *On Gardens*. He not only recommends those plants that "unfold their greatest beauty" for each particular month of the year, he also describes an ideal garden consisting of both a geometrically laid-out and a "wild" half, that is nevertheless carefully composed: "Truly princely gardens (...) should cover an area of no less than thirty acres of land and be divided into three sections: a lawn at the entrance, a meadow or wilderness in the background and the principal garden at the centre, moreover avenues on both sides." He also stresses the importance of engaging all the senses: "Since the scent of flowers in the air, where it wafts to and fro like music streaming (through the air), is far more lovely than in one's hand, one can easily enjoy this pleasure by getting to know those flowers and plants that fill the air with delicious aromas." Thus the white violet, the musk rose, carnations, lime blossoms, honeysuckle and strawberry leaves emanate "a most delicious, hearty scent as they wilt".

1628: TOMB GARDENS IV In his stylistically influential work *Architectura civilis,* the German Renaissance architect and garden designer Joseph Furttenbach (1591–1667) speaks of a cemetery as a garden. The German word for cemetery *Friedhof,* originally designated any enclosed space, forecourt of a house or a garden. Once it is consecrated, this space becomes a burial site, a place of peace. However, it is only in the course of the 18th century that cemeteries become part of garden design, when the American concept of *lawn cemeteries* begins to take hold in England. Flowers are often regarded as too cheerful; the design should reflect the solemn character of the site. Nevertheless, many urban cemeteries are planned with a view to future use as a public park, as demonstrated by the German architect Johann Michael Voit (1771–1846) in his book *Über die Anlegung und Umwandlung der Gottesäcker in heitere Ruhegärten der Abgeschiedenen* (On the Layout and Conversion of Graveyards into Cheerful Gardens of Tranquillity and Peace), published in 1825. In cities today, cemeteries are not only places that offer tranquillity; they are much needed "green lungs" for the population plagued by noise and exhaust fumes.

Tulip hysteria and stock-market crash: *Parisian Option* (colour print, 2007) from the photo series *Bullish on Bulbs* by the Swiss artist Rémy Markowitsch. The image was created by "transluminating" a book page to produce a superimposition of the front and back sides.

1637: SPECULATION The market for tulip bulbs collapses in the crash at the stock exchange in the Netherlands. The longstanding passion for tulip bulbs imported from Asia Minor and the Middle East, rarities and hence all the more sought after, leads to increasingly unfettered speculation with the bulbs. Soon the prices and the real value are no longer in any healthy relationship: in 1636 a single bulb is said to have reached the price of a new coach with two horses complete with tackle, and very rare specimens would cost the equivalent of 50 000 euros today. More and more people – from farmhand to nobleman – invest their money, hoping for a quick return. However, when the first investors fail to secure their profit, they unleash a wave of panic sales causing the speculation bubble to pop and the entire trade to collapse. With his photo series *Bullish on Bulbs* (2007), the Swiss artist Rémy Markowitsch (*1957) photographed the tulip obsession at the time and the stock market crash and set it in relationship to the present: in today's stock market language, "bullish" identifies the atmosphere when the rates are rising. His seductive tulip photos *American Option* and *Parisian Option* stand for the enduring greed for quick profit – and for possible failure.

AFTER 1648: TREE NURSERY After the end of the Thirty Years' War a rejuvenation of the forests in Europe begins by means of seedlings; the excessive use of wood in the Middle Ages has become painfully apparent. For one, certain types of trees are used as building material, for another, reforestation is meant to counter the drying-up and erosion. The first systematically operated *nurseries* arise on the outskirts of parks near royal houses, where also fruit trees and box and yew trees are cultivated, which are suitable for *topiary*.

Around 1900 the Späth nursery founded by the garden designer and botanist Franz Ludwig Späth (1839–1913) in front of Berlin's gates was considered the largest arboretum in the world; circa 1930, around 4000 different types of trees are listed. After heavy damage to the grounds in the Second World War and the transfer of private property to state-owned property in East Germany in 1947, the *Späth-Arboretum* now belongs to Humboldt University in Berlin. The *tree nurseries* and garden shops develop to become today's garden centres, which offer everything that the heart of a hobby gardener desires, from pruning shears to bulb planters. Also mail-order shopping for seeds, bulbs, fertiliser, tools and garden furniture experiences a steady boom.

| 1742: IMPORT II

FROM 1655: ORANGERY The yearning for southern landscapes and the aroma of orange and lemon blossoms, gives rise to the first *orangeries*. To begin with the term is only used to designate the location where orange and lemon trees, hibiscus or pomegranate trees are set out in pots in summer time. Then, greenhouses are built to protect the sensitive plants against frost. These structures stand empty in summer when they are used as ballrooms. The French physicist and engineer Salomon de Caus speaks of a "pomegranate house" in the castle park at Heidelberg as early as 1620. Citrus fruit is not the only type of plant that is cultivated in the *orangery;* myrrh, laurel, oleander and roses are also grown there. Moreover, this era witnesses the true science of propagation, re-potting and grafting. Significant *orangeries,* among others, are the Zwinger in Dresden, the Lower Belvedere in Vienna and the *orangery* in Kassel.

1652: BRODERIE The French garden designer Claude Mollet's (1563–1650) *Le théâtre des plans et jardinages* is published posthumously. The dynasty of royal gardeners begins with his father, Jacques, and is continued by his son André, who works in Sweden for Queen Christine (1626–1689) where he writes the book *Le jardin de plaisir.* Claude Mollet is the author of the *compartiment en broderie,* ornamental beds that appear like needlepoint or *broderie.* He works in the *Tuileries,* in Versailles, Fontainebleau or Saint-Germain-en-Laye, where he is said to have followed André Le Nôtre's plans. In 1685, the Huguenot Daniel Marot (1661–1752) flees from France to Holland. With his *parterres en broderies* composed of various types of gravel and artfully trimmed box arabesques, he invests the royal park of Het Loo near Apeldoorn with a Baroque charm and transforms it into one of the most important gardens in Europe. When William III of Orange (1650–1702) and Princess Royal Mary II (1662–1694) are crowned King and Queen of England in 1689, they are no doubt one of many sources

Like embroidery: parterre garden in the royal park of Het Loo,
Apeldoorn, Holland

that bring a Dutch influence to the garden arts in England. From 1970 to 1984, the transformations undertaken in Het Loo over the course of the 19th and 20th centuries are reversed and the symmetrical axial ensemble is reconstructed to the condition circa 1700.

1664: INSPIRATION V Jean-Baptiste Lully (1632–1687), a composer and dancer born in Italy who would have a brilliant career in the court of Louis XIV, composes *Les plaisirs de l'île enchantée (The Pleasures of the Enchanted Island)* for an open-air performance in the park of Versailles; the author of the text for the piece is Molière (1622–1673). The ballet comedy is a great success, thus further Lully-Molière co-operations are performed, such as *Le Mariage forcé* and *La Princesse d'Elide,* which both tell of secret, amorous meetings in grottoes and temples and are inspired by the royal garden. After the open-air performances, however, the gardener apparently had to work for days to clear away the devastation of the beds, lawns and paths caused by the many enthusiastic guests.

1680: SCIENCE II The German natural scientist and flower painter Maria Sibylla Merian (1647–1717) writes the *Neues Blumenbuch* (New Book of Flowers), which is first published in three individual volumes from 1675 onwards. Merian is not only a highly precise watercolourist, she is also knowledgeable in printing techniques and therefore able to self-publish her studies in book form. From 1699 to 1701 she leaves on a research expedition to Suriname (South America) to study and paint insects and plants. She publishes the results of her observations in 1705 under the title *Metamorphosis insectorum Surinamensium.*

1689: TOPIARY II The French gardener Guillaume Beaumont (1650–1729), who is active in England from 1680 to 1727, plants the garden of the manor house Levens Hall in the English county of Cumbria from 1689 to 1712. From the middle of the 18th century, *topiary* became less fashionable, yet the garden at Levens Hall nonetheless survives, and Alexander Forbes renovates it from 1810 to 1862. The yews, some of which are 300 years old, clipped in geometric shapes or in the form

Spirals, spheres, cones: *topiary* in the *Victorian Garden* of Levens Hall, Kendal, Cumbria, England

of chess figures, the hedgerow of beech and the supported box trees are an outstanding example of the art of topiary. The American landscape architect Martha Schwartz (*1950) quotes the cut forms in the rooftop garden of the Whitehead Institute for Biomedical Research, Cambridge, Massachusetts – these *topiary* however, are made of plastic. | 1980: INSTANT GARDEN

1715: AMPHITHEATRE III Work begins on the *Claremont Landscape Garden* around the Palladian Claremont House near Esher in the county of Surrey in England. The property of the National Trust | 1895: LARGEST GARDEN OWNER since 1949, the magnificent park represents the intellectual and conceptual methods of seminal park designers, such as Charles Bridgeman, Lancelot "Capability" Brown (1716–1783) and William Kent (1685–1748). An amphitheatre with a view over the lake forms the centre of the park. People in fancy dress gather at the Claremont Fête Champêtre annual garden festival to listen to concerts and experience theatre shows and fireworks.

1728: ANTIQUITY REDISCOVERED II Robert Castell's (?–1729) book *The Villas of the Ancients Illustrated* is published in England, containing reconstructive illustrations of the villas and gardens of Pliny the Younger. | 97–107: VISTA The book reflects the renewed interest in Antiquity and the importance of classic Roman culture for English garden design.

1729: MONASTERY GARDEN II, LANDSCAPE PARK II After a fire, the buildings and gardens of the Benedictine monastery of Engelberg are rebuilt and expanded in the process. The monks create a fish pond outside the monastery boundaries, complete with a pavilion and terrace, bowling lane and walking paths: their awareness of the beauty of the environment transforms the landscape into a landscape park, probably unique in Switzerland at that time. As in many monasteries, the monastery nursery grows vegetables, herbs and flowers for their own use as well as seedlings and potted plants for sale.

Antiquity rediscovered: the Palladian Bridge in the park of Stowe House
northeast of Oxford, England. Stowe was never only a garden:
it also stands for (political) ideas and is full of allusions to Greek mythology.

View into the agricultural used landscape and "wild" nature.
In the *Pashley Manor Gardens* in Sussex, England,
a ditch or "ha-ha" prevents sheep from getting into the garden.

1735: THE GRACES OF WILDERNESS I William Kent assumes the task of designing the garden at Stowe in the county of Buckinghamshire in central England. The "foe of all straight lines", as the painter, architect and garden designer is also known, creates this garden as an idyllic, painterly image of nature, thus setting a new standard. There are groups of trees loosely distributed across broad stretches of lawn, a small valley with a Palladian-style temple as an *Elysian Field* and a *ha-ha* (or *ah-ah* or *aha*), that is, a ditch not visible from the garden, and therefore presenting a surprise: ha ha! This extends the garden optically into the surroundings, which are used for agriculture, and prevents cows and sheep from entering the garden itself. Later still, artificial ruins or follies become typical elements of the English landscape park. England has evolved into the most liberal country in Europe: industrial revolution, civic liberty and education and at the same time a yearning for nature, grandeur, and sensibility as well as a sense of drama romanticise these gardens. William Kent redesigned Charles Bridgeman's landscape garden at Rousham House in the county of Oxfordshire in 1738 – already then, it was considered one of the most beautiful gardens of its era. Strolling through the park, visitors experience it as a succession of stage-like scenarios.

The philosopher and poet Jean-Jacques Rousseau (1712–1778) is not the only one with a desire to return to an intimate connection with nature; the natural philosopher, the Earl of Shaftesbury (1671–1713) has coined the phrase of the "graces of the wilderness" and ridicules the "formal mockery of princely gardens" in France, greatly influencing the design of gardens in England. Alexander Pope (1688–1744), the poet, finally joins forces with Joseph Addison (1672–1719) to publish an article on garden planning in the *Spectator*, after which he creates his own legendary "wild" garden in Twickenham devoid of all geometrical design. Also the "wilderness", which is staged in a section of the large landscape park *Prior Park* near Bath, built between 1734 and 1764, can be traced back to the influence of Pope. The entrepreneur and philanthropist Ralph Allen (1694–1764) created the park with its gentle grass slopes, a grotto, lake and Palladian bridge, presumably based on advice from Lancelot "Capability" Brown.

1742: IMPORT II The German composer Georg Philipp Telemann (1681–1767) creates a list of plants in his garden, the *Garten = Vorraht (garden = inventory)*. Among the roughly seventy listed plants are tulips, hyacinths, narcissi, bellflowers, carnations, peonies, nasturtia and cornflowers. Telemann is especially fascinated by peonies. His "love for flowers" leads him to appoint extensive studies in search of new and exotic plants. He contacts famous botanists, such as Albrecht von Haller (1708–1777) from Switzerland, and musicians who are also garden enthusiasts, such as Johann Georg Pisendel (1687–1755) at Dresdner Hof, Georg Friedrich Händel (1685–1759) in London and Carl Philipp Emanuel Bach (1714–1788) in Berlin. | 1749: INSPIRATION VI Von Haller sends Telemann rare seeds, Pisendel sends him exotic cacti and aloes. In addition, Telemann studies the mail-order catalogues of the then famous *Caspar Bosischen Garten* in Leipzig run by the gardener Johann Ernst Probst (?–1782).

1747: RUINS In *Hagley Park* near the Palladian manor Hagley Hall in the English county of Worcestershire, the Neo-Gothic architect and landscape architect Sanderson Miller (1716–1780) built imitation castle ruins. In keeping with the general interest in classical Antiquity archaeology, it was fashionable to indulge in the romantic view of ruins in the features of large parks, and to set all sorts of castle, abbey and column remains within the garden as motifs of the ephemeral and sublime. This was also the case in *Strawberry Hill Park* around Horace Walpole's (1717–1797) villa in Twickenham near London, where the master of the house had a Gothic ruin, a Palladian bridge and a Chinese pagoda built. Additional imitation ruins were created in 1748, among others, in the park of the Sanssouci palace in Potsdam and, in 1790, the so-called Löwenburg or lion's castle was built in the *Schlosspark Wilhelmshöhe* in Kassel.

1749: INSPIRATION VI Georg Friedrich Händel's *Music for the Royal Fireworks* premiered in *Green Park* in London – with a huge orchestra, but still without the string section that Händel wanted. Fifty-seven musicians – twenty-four oboes, twelve bassoons, nine horns, nine trumpets and three pairs of kettle drums – play at the public dress rehearsal on 21 April 1749, in *Vauxhall Gardens;* 12000 spectators attempt to listen to the music; a traffic jam forms on London Bridge. Händel's *Music for the Royal Fireworks* remains the largest garden concert in history until 1974, when the American composer Leonard Bernstein (1918–1990) played symphonies by Gustav Mahler (1860–1911) at an open-air concert in New York's *Central Park* with the New York Philharmonic. Whether Claude Debussy's (1862–1918) piano piece *Jardins sous la pluie,* inspired by the garden of the Villa Medici in Rome, or Olivier Messiaen's (1908–1992) *Jardin du sommeil d'amour,* whether brass bands playing in pavilions or accordion players and singers with guitars performing on Sunday afternoons in public parks: music is composed for gardens and garden parties; gardens inspire compositions, and the rumour is that plants grow better to certain sounds.

1741 TO 1780: INSPIRATION VII With *Stourhead Garden* in the county of Wiltshire in England, the banker Henry Hoare II (1705–1785) has one of the most outstanding English landscape parks laid out. Paths around the lake at the centre of the park lead strollers through the diversely designed man-made landscape. *Views* – views of the landscape resembling paintings – fill the spirit with calm and inspiration. Various references to classical Greek and Italian culture, such as the Pantheon, the Temple of Apollo and a Palladian bridge, let visitors to the garden imagine themselves in a newly created Arcadia. Great influence came from the paintings of Claude Lorrain (1600–1682) and Nicolas Poussin (1594–1665), which romanticise the Roman and Greek landscapes, and from the wild landscapes by Salvator Rosa (1615–1673). Also fashionable is the *Claude Glass,* a round, tinted and convexly curved mirror. This is held up to the eye in such a way that it is possible to see the landscape behind one's back, which in the mirror looks like an Arcadian landscape by Claude Lorrain. This perception decisively shapes garden design: groups of trees and bushes, lakes and paths are staged with an awareness of space, of depth and colours, foreground and background, in short: like paintings.

At *Stourhead,* like in many other landscape parks in the south of England – for instance, in *Lanhydrock House and Garden* in Cornwall –

English landscape park par excellence: *Stourhead Garden,* Stourton, Wiltshire, England, with Palladian bridge and Pantheon

blooming in May are huge rhododendrons, azaleas and magnolias, which were introduced from North America beginning in the mid-19th century. One can walk like an ant through tunnels cut in the branches of the rhododendrons. On a stroll around the lake and over the gentle hill, both static and dynamic moments are experienced: resting, one has a view of the space, which functions like a painting; while walking, one experiences a succession of images and spaces. In the English landscape park, painting and garden design, culture and nature, rest, intellectual contemplation and physical movement come together to form a gesamtkunstwerk.

Also in the Japanese *strolling gardens,* which are already popular beginning in the 13th century, one follows a carefully laid-out path and is refreshed by varied perspectives. These *views* follow from one another like landscape scenes on a long picture scroll.

FROM 1750: SYMBOL OF FREEDOM AND INSPIRATION VIII Marie Antoinette (1755–1793), wife of King Louis XVI, has an English-style landscape park created around the small palace Petit Trianon in the park of Versailles: the *Petit Parc* are the most significant grounds of this type in France. In 2005, Marie Antoinette's favourite tree, an oak with a trunk width of five metres, has to be cut down. The idea of the English landscape garden spreads further on the Continent based on Rousseau's philosophy: consciously designed but nonetheless not geometrically-hierarchically rigid, this type of garden corresponds with the need for more "naturalness" and reflects social and political upheavals. Although the major parks are still created by wealthy aristocrats, the new type of garden of the English landscape park opposes the symbolism of absolutist power of the (French) Baroque garden and is thereby also an anti-aristocratic symbol of freedom.

Additional significant French landscape gardens are the *Jardins d'Ermenonville,* which arose between 1763 and 1776, the garden *Désert de Retz* near Yvelines, and the *Parc Monceau,* which was designed from 1774 to 1782 with Gothic ruins, temples and *chinoiserie. Parc Monceau,* redesigned by Scottish garden architect Thomas Blaikie (1750–1838) in an English style from 1785 to 1788, is currently a popular green oasis

Palace for palms: *The Tropical House, Kew Gardens,*
painting by Thomas Greenhalgh, 1884

in the middle of Paris. The environmental researcher and writer Jean-Jacques Rousseau died in Ermenonville in 1778, therefore, the southern part is now named *Parc Jean-Jacques Rousseau.*

1752: ZOOLOGICAL GARDEN Austrian Emperor Franz I founded the *Tiergarten* or zoo in the park of Schönbrunn Palace. Along with the *Ménagerie du Jardin des Plantes* in Paris (1793), it is considered the oldest still existing zoo in the world and has been open to the public since 1778. Although archaeological discoveries in Upper Egypt do provide evidence of the keeping of elephants and wildcats already circa 3500 BC, zoological gardens or zoos in today's sense – park-like facilities with enclosures for animals – first developed in the waning 18th century: the exhibition and the study of animals come together, whereby entirely spectacular landscapes are created with man-made mountains and rock landscapes – for instance, at the Budapest zoo, which opened in 1866. Nowadays, zoos attempt to re-create the most natural possible living spaces for the animals, where they can also hide from visitors in the thicket of plants.

1759: SCIENCE III AND GLASS HOUSE I The *Royal Botanic Gardens* are created at the former summer residence of the Royal Family at Kew in southwestern London and are completed in 1761 by the addition of one of the most architecturally significant *orangeries* of the time. The gardens, which are now famous throughout the world and a Unesco World Heritage site, offer unique botanic diversity on an area of 121 hectares and in the stately glasshouses – the *Palm House,* the *Waterlily House* and the *Temperate House* with plants from South Africa, America, Asia and the world's tallest glasshouse-raised Chilean wine palm. Also open since 2005 is *Davies Alpine House,* a glass house with alpine plants.

FROM 1764: LANDSCAPE PARK III Lancelot "Capability" Brown (1716–1783), who sets out by working with William Kent at *Stowe Landscape Gardens,* advances to become England's busiest garden designer. His nickname reflects his talent for coming up with design ideas for even the most challenging topographies. The reconfiguration

Tree groups on open lawn areas: *clumps* in the *Woodland Garden*
at Antony House, Torpoint, Cornwall, England

of the garden at Blenheim Palace in the English county of Oxford-shire occupies him for a full decade: from 1764 onwards, he begins to replace the Baroque garden with lawns, diverts the flow of the River Glyme and creates a dam and two lakes with undulating shore-lines. Establishing so-called *clumps* can be traced back to Brown, individual groups of trees that are set into open lawns as eye-catching focal points. Brown is said to have designed nearly 300 parks in England and rejected one commission from abroad with the reason that he "hasn't completed England yet". From circa 1760 onwards, he begins to transform the French-inspired garden at Chatsworth House in the county of Derbyshire, created by George London (circa 1650–1714) and Henry Wise (1653–1738), into a landscape park and to expand it; once again he builds a dam on a river, creating a lake, erects a Palladian bridge and thus creates a harmonious link between the park with its Baroque core and the environs of the estate.

1776: GARDEN PLANNING Lancelot "Capability" Brown and the garden designer Humphry Repton (1752–1818) collaborate on the design of a vast landscape garden called *Sheffield Park* in Sussex, including a series of lakes. Repton becomes known for his emphasis on the *genius loci* and his *Red Books:* he painted watercolour views of the existing and new gardens for his clients based on the before-and-after principle in books bound in red leather; his plans were additionally visualised by means of overlays. The combination of gardens in the Tudor style or based on the medieval model near the house and a landscape park is adopted as the fashionable style and Repton's writings influence German garden architects that come after him, such as Prince Pückler-Muskau. | 1834: LANDSCAPE PARK V

Humphry Repton also designed the *Russell Square Garden* in London, Bloomsbury, circa 1800. Fenced *garden squares* can still be found throughout London: some are public, some private, and the residents have a key to the small parks in the middle of their squares formed by rows of buildings and streets. At the end of the 18th century, cows grazed in many *garden squares* – for example, on Leicester Square – and people hung their washing to dry over the bushes. Today they are green havens.

1777/1778: ARCADES II Among many other topics, the poet Johann Wolfgang von Goethe (1749–1832) was also keen on garden design. Supported by his client Duke Karl August von Sachsen-Weimar (1757–1828), he designed the *Park an der Ilm*, an ideal Arcadian landscape around the Ilm River; it is his largest garden design project.

1779: GARDENING TIPS III *The Planter's Guide* by the gardener James Meader is published in London. The handbook lists numerous types of trees and makes suggestions for planting a garden. The pharmacist and botanist William Curtis (1746–1799) launches the *Botanical Magazine* in monthly issues, each of which contains three hand-coloured engravings of newly cultivated plants. This is followed in 1822 by the gardening magazine *Encyclopedia of Gardening* published by the garden theoretician and author John Claudius Loudon (1783–1843), who is very much involved in the evolution of glass greenhouses and in 1826 by his *Gardener's Magazine*, with the aim of promoting the intellect and character of garden lovers. From 1850 onwards, the *Gardeners' Chronicle*, the *Journal of the Horticultural Society of London* (today: *The Garden*) and the *Cottage Gardener* are available at newsstands.

With the strengthening of the middle class in Europe and the construction of middle-class homes and villas, the interest in designing one's own garden also grew, which precipitated a boom of how-to literature providing practical advice. Several books are evidence of this, such as Carl Hampel's (1849–1930) *Hundert kleine Gärten: Plan, Beschreibung und Bepflanzung, entworfen und bearbeitet für Gärtner, Baumeister und Villenbesitzer*, published in Berlin in 1894, or Hermann Jäger's (1815–1890) *Ideenmagazin zur zweckmässigsten Anlegung und Ausstattung geschmackvoller Hausgärten und anderer kleiner Gartenanlagen*, published in Weimar in 1845. Today, too, magazines on garden design are among the crisis-resistant print media. | 1968: GARDEN TIPS V

1779–1785: PUBLIC PARKS III Christian Cay Lorenz Hirschfeld (1742–1792), German philosopher and garden theoretician, publishes his five-volume *Theorie der Gartenkunst* (Theory on Garden Art). It is the first comprehensive reference work on gardens.

102

Between Enlightenment and Romanticism: Rousseau Island in *Wörlitzer Park*, Germany. Like other Rousseau Islands, it is modelled on the cenotaph of Jean-Jacques Rousseau on the *Île des peupliers* (Poplar Island) in *Jardins d'Ermenonville*, France.

Hirschfeld's thoughts on the aesthetic of the *public park*, which should serve for the recreation and education of the urban population, decisively influence the development of this type of garden.

1790: LANDSCAPE PARK IV AND ARTIFICIAL MOUN-TAIN II The English landscape garden *Wörlitzer Park*, commissioned by Prince Leopold Friedrich Franz von Anhalt-Dessau (1740–1817), is already a sight worth seeing shortly after its completion; it is considered the first English garden in Continental Europe; since 2000 it has been among the Unesco World Heritage sites. The prince attempted to develop a scholarly state, inviting painters, poets and philosophers, and among other things, creates a library for garden design. He considers his garden as the aesthetic centre of an enlightened state. At the middle of Lake Wörlitz lies the *Rousseau Island* along whose shores walkers come across a *nymphaeum*, a pavilion in the style of a small temple and the Gothic House. The combination of Classicist, Neo-Gothic and Neo-Romanesque architecture is unified into a whole through the garden. In the summer of 2005, after a long break and elaborate renovation, the *Vesuv von Wörlitz* installed on the artificial rocky island *Stein* is back in operation: from time to time, it is allowed to "erupt" with fireworks, bonfires, smoke and rolls of thunder, and in summer 2007 with a "terrifying explosion" by the Swiss artist Roman Signer (*1938).

1794: INSPIRATION IX The English poet and painter William Blake (1757–1827) published the poem *The Garden of Love* as part of the poem cycle *Songs of Innocence and Experience*. Blake thematized the naturalness of sexual love by describing the spiritual transformation from child to mature adult and Catholic morals as suppression of sexual pleasure. The garden or simply the green of the surroundings is the symbol for the innocent, paradisiacal connection to nature: "I went to the Garden of Love, / And saw what I never had seen: / A Chapel was built in the midst, / Where I used to play on the green. / And the gates of this Chapel were shut, / And *Thou shalt not.* writ / over the door; / So I turn'd to the Garden of Love, / That so many sweet flowers bore. And I saw it was filled with graves, / And tomb-stones where

Exporting the English landscape park: the *Englische Garten*
in Munich, Germany

flowers should be: / And Priests in black gowns, were walking their rounds, / And binding with briars, my joys & desires." The garden as a symbol of the utopia of a paradisiacal state or as a backdrop for the emotions and spiritual constitution of protagonists is a recurring motif in literature until today.

1799: PUBLIC PARKS IV Following extensive study journeys through France and England, where he meets Lancelot "Capability" Brown and others, Friedrich Ludwig von Sckell (1750–1823) redesigns the *Englische Garten* in Munich into a public park upon commission from the Elector of Bavaria. This project marks the beginning of the planning of urban green spaces that are open to the public. Sckell hoped that his park would "serve for the cosy and gregarious rapprochement of all classes of society, who meet here in the lap of beautiful nature". Pavilions are also built in many public parks, where music groups play on Sundays: march, dance and operetta music are popular.

CIRCA 1800: ECCENTRICS The Romantic park of Fonthill Abbey, a Neo-Gothic country estate in south England's Wiltshire, part abbey, part fortress, is as eccentric as its immeasurably wealthy owner William Beckford (1759–1844), who seeks refuge on his estate from persecution for his homosexual orientation. Surrounded by a 3-metre-high and 12-kilometre-long wall, he promotes the growth of a controlled wilderness in which animals find sanctuary from the hunt. Beckford's agents purchase large trees, shrubs and plants in the colonies and in a letter to his mother he boasts of having "planted more than one million trees within a single year". In 1822, Fonthill Abbey is auctioned off at Christie's in London for 330 000 pounds; several years later, the abbey tower collapses. Today, the garden is in ruins, though it is possible to visit the chapel and Lancaster Tower. Joseph Mallord William Turner (1775–1851), who resided in Fonthill Abbey in 1799, paints the view of Fonthill from a stone quarry.

1800 ALPINUM I The Scot Alexander Nasmyth (1758–1840) is one of the first to create an *alpinum* (alpine garden) in England. Soon

Protection for plants, animals and landscape: the *Swiss National Park*
established in 1914, Zernez in the Engadin

after, Peter Joseph Lenné (1789–1866), the German Classicist garden architect par excellence, adds an *alpinum* to the castle park at Sanssouci in Potsdam. In 1870, the Irish gardener and garden journalist William Robinson (1838–1935), publisher of the journal *The Wild Garden*, propagates the idea of creating rock gardens with alpine flowers in England in his book *Alpine Flowers for Gardens*. Over the course of the 19th century, (English) enthusiasm for the Alps increases steadily. Switzerland and the alpine flora attain cult status and *Swiss gardens* are planted also in locations that are hardly suitable for alpine plants.

| 1880: ALPINUM II

1804: ROYAL HORTICULTURAL SOCIETY AND GARDEN EXHIBITION I Sir Joseph Banks (1743–1820) and John Wedgwood found the London Horticultural Society in London, which is elevated to Royal Horticultural Society by Prince Albert (1819–1861) in 1861. The *RHS* promotes and preserves knowledge on plants and garden culture, mounts garden exhibitions, of which the Chelsea Flower Show and the flower shows at Hampton Court and Tatton Park are world-famous. It also owns four gardens: *Wisley* in Surrey, *Rosemoor* in Devon, *Hyde Hall* in Essex and *Harlow Carr* in North Yorkshire – and administers the Lindley Library, which was established on the basis of the library of the botanist John Lindley (1799–1865).

1810: NATIONAL PARK The English poet William Wordsworth (1770–1850) calls for the creation of a national park, in which plants and animals are protected from humankind. The idea of preserving natural landscapes of extraordinary beauty for posterity is also pursued in 1832 by the American painter George Catlin (1796–1872) and in 1880 by Baron Adolf Erik von Nordenskiöld (1832–1901) in Sweden. Europe's first national park is thus inaugurated in Sweden in 1909, followed by a national park in Switzerland in 1914. In the U.S., the American landscape photographer Ansel Adams (1902–1984) becomes a key supporter with his black-and-white photos that mediate the untouched, breathtaking beautiful nature in the national parks. Today, some 120 countries have a total of at least 2220 national parks in which a wide variety of landscapes, fauna and flora are protected.

Safe wilderness, rare microclimate: *Trebah* and *Glendurgan* gardens,
Falmouth, Cornwall, England,
feature plants originating from subtropical environments

西神苑

平安神宮が創建された次明治二十八年に
中神苑とともに造られた。
中神苑を中心とし、池の西御に
日龍池をやどし火島・北島とは
出島・北島には神苑唯一の滝があり
西側の葉山には本殿（隆地學）がある。
初夏を彩る池畔の是菖蒲は特に有名
である。
（約二百種類、約二千株植栽）

Renowned are, for example, *Yellowstone National Park* (1872) and *Yosemite National Park* (1890) in the U.S., *Serengeti National Park* (1951) in Tanzania and *Parque Nacional Galápagos* in Ecuador (1959).

1820: THE GRACES OF WILDERNESS II The shipowner Alfred Fox and his wife, Sarah, purchase a cottage near Durgan, Cornwall, and begin to create a truly paradisiacal garden in a small valley; they christen the garden *Glendurgan,* a composite of the name of the town and the name of their first dog Glen. The valley, where *Glendurgan* is laid out, slopes down to the Helford River, which, in turn, flows into the nearby ocean; thanks to the Gulf Stream and its sheltered location, the valley is a rare curiosity of nature: a nearly subtropical microclimate. Through the shipping company, the Foxes have connections to Africa and Asia and instruct their captains to bring back plants and seeds, which flourish extremely well in this, for England highly unusual, climate. Tree-ferns and palm trees grow, although Sarah Fox's orchard of lemon, orange and apple trees no longer exists. In 1833 they plant a laurel bush maze. *Glendurgan* is a controlled jungle forest of imported plants, influenced by the Romantic idea of the beautiful savage. Strolling beneath the massive rhododendron, or bamboo, it is easy to indulge in contemplation without having to fear being devoured by a lion: the wilderness has been freed of its horrors. Here, magnolias and camellias flourish, there are cypresses, cedars and pines, water lilies and irises, and at the bottom of the valley grows the giant rhubarb with its huge leaves. In the Bible-inspired section of the garden, the *Holy Corner* visitors find an olive tree, a thorn bush, a yew and a Judas tree. Aside from *Glendurgan,* the gardens at *Trebah* and *Trengwainton,* also in Cornwall, and the *Tresco Abbey Gardens* on the Isles of Scilly are distinguished by a similarly lush vegetation.

1822: GARDEN GNOMES In his *Encyclopedia of Gardening,* John Claudius Loudon | 1779: GARDEN TIPS IV promotes the idea of animating gardens with garden gnomes. As early as 1744 to 1750, the manufacture of porcelain garden gnomes reaches a high point through the production at the Imperial Manufacturer in Vienna; however, it is Sir

Charles Edmund Isham (1819–1903) who is credited with launching and popularising the idea of decorating gardens with gnomes, which had disappeared from the scene after the Baroque. The little gnomes and hobgoblins, taken from fairy tales and legends, make a comeback as lovable kitsch figures and are still today found in front yards and allotments, mostly in plastic. The *Gnome Reserve and Wild Flower Garden*, a garden with some 1000 garden gnomes in the county of Devon in southern England, is regarded as the El Dorado of garden gnomes.

1824: RESTORATION I In Berlin, Peter Joseph Lenné is appointed Royal Director of Gardens. He converts the gardens at Sanssouci, at Charlottenhof and Glienicke in Potsdam into landscape gardens – all are now Unesco World Heritage sites – and transforms Berlin's *Große Tiergarten* in a country park from 1833 to 1840. In *Klein-Glienicke*, Lenné plants some 25000 trees; the works are completed in 1860. However, decay has already begun to set in a few years before his death. From 1930 onwards, roads linking Potsdam with Berlin are laid through the park, and a youth hostel is later installed in the castle. Interest in the heritage is only reawakened in 1979, after which castle and park are restored. Gardens need people who take care of them, otherwise their special spirit disappears, and it takes years of work to bring them back to life: for the American poet Emily Dickinson (1830–1886), her garden was her personal paradise and source of inspiration for poems and impressions that often revolve around mortality and the desire for love. Her garden remained untended after her death and was ultimately destroyed by a hurricane in 1938. It is now restored and part of the Emily Dickinson Museum in Amherst, Massachusetts. Similarly, *The Lost Gardens of Heligan* in Cornwall, which reached their peak of beauty at the end of the 19th century, were left to their own devices for decades; in 1990, a storm dealt them a final blow. But Sir Tim Smit (*1954) and a group of volunteers have restored *Heligan Gardens* in ten years of back-breaking work; now, the *Wall Garden*, the *Jungle* with palm trees and bamboo, *The Lost Valley* and a decorative garden with grotto, pond and huge rhododendrons are flourishing once again.

Mechanical garden work: the first lawnmower is a spindle mower.

1830: LAWNMOWER The British textile engineer Edwin
Beard Budding (1795–1846) invents the lawnmower, which is introduced
in The *Gardener's Magazine* in 1832. The ideal lawn, which should
be dense and devoid of weeds and flowers, must be mowed regularly
and to this end the large *tapis vert* or the *pleasure grounds* in English
landscape gardens are laboriously mowed with scythes: at Blenheim
Palace, fifty employees are said to have been occupied with mowing
the grass in the park. Increasingly popular sports such as tennis,
football and cricket also require large expanses of lawn – and more
rational mowing methods are therefore in high demand when Budding
makes the discovery in a commercial mill that the principle of a
machine which moves the finished cloth past a rotating spindle with
blades to trim any protruding fibres can also be applied to cutting
grass. The British firm Ransomes manufactures the spindle mower
from 1836 onwards, and also introduces the first motorised lawnmower to the market in 1902. From 1956 onwards, the German firm
Solo sells a sickle mower, the principle of which becomes the standard
on the Continent while spindle mowers continue to be more common
in England. Psychologists consider mowing the lawn on Saturdays
to be a relaxing ritual after a hard week of work. Since 1995, however,
robotic lawnmowers have whirred on their own around the garden
regardless of the day of the week.

1834: LANDSCAPE PARK V The richly illustrated book
Andeutungen über Landschaftsgärtnerei by Prince Hermann Ludwig
Heinrich von Pückler-Muskau (1785–1871) is published in Stuttgart. In
Muskau, in the current border region between Germany and Poland,
he transforms the landscape, including the villages and the village
of Muskau into a huge landscape park; the park is currently listed as a
Unesco World Heritage site. The setting even includes a distillery, a
wax factory and a mine. However, when he overextends himself finan-
cially and has to sell the estate in 1845, he moves into the castle he
inherited, Branitz near Cottbus, where he once again begins to transform the abandoned garden into an idyllic landscape garden, giving
rise to *Fürst-Pückler-Park*. He remodels the grounds, creates a *pleasure ground* and heaps earth into mountain-like pyramids both on

Space for private enjoyment of the garden and a source of fruit,
vegetables and flowers: allotment, ca. 1900

land and in the lake, which are intended as burial sites for him and his wife; the park has been restored since 2015. Additionally, he plants roughly 300 000 trees and a rose arbour. Although he calls the garden that is close to the castle an "extended living space", he sees the park as "concentrated, idealised nature". In his book he also explains the term "pleasure ground" as: "This means a piece of land adjacent to a house, which is fenced in and ornamented, of much greater extent than gardens, and something of an intermediate thing, a connecting element between the park and the actual gardens." The politically liberal prince, who undertook extended journeys and also made a name for himself as a writer, went down in the history of garden culture as an ingenious designer of two of the most important landscape parks in Germany.

During the Second World War, battles take place in Muskau and the garden is largely destroyed and divided into Polish and German sections by establishing a border along the River Neisse; today, Muskau has been restored and remains a cross-border connection straddling the two countries.

FROM 1844: ALLOTMENT The German physician and pedagogue Daniel Gottlieb Moritz Schreber (1808–1861) is appointed director of an orthopaedic clinic. He designs playgrounds with small gardens for children and adults, which evolve into allotment clubs thanks to the efforts of his son-in-law E. I. Hauschild in 1864. The small allotment parcels complete with sheds provide vegetables, fruit and flowers and are thus a valuable source of provisions.

Today referred to as small or family gardens, they also serve as an evening or weekend refuge for people without a property of their own. The cliché of the respectable, meticulously tended garden plagued by petty disagreements between neighbours, in which the national flag is often seen to flutter in the wind in Switzerland, has in the meantime been countered by a multicultural blend of nations and a growing number of organic gardeners.

1848: PUBLIC PARKS V Andrew J. Downing (1815–1852), an American landscape gardener and editor of the journal *The Horticul-*

Agriculture for the family table: dacha with garden outside Olonets,
a small town 300 kilometres northeast of St. Petersburg, Olonetsky District, Russia

Fruit and vegetable garden for evenings and weekends:
allotment in Wipkingen, Zurich, Switzerland.
Also referred to as small gardens, *family gardens* or *Pünten*

Open spaces for walks, jogging and picnics:
Kensington Gardens and directly adjacent *Hyde Park*, London, England

turist travels to Germany and is so impressed by the *Englische Garten* in Munich that he prompts the creation of New York's *Central Park*: "As backward as the Germans may be in things political in general, they are no doubt progressive in their approach to public parks. It truly contains a piece of democracy that would be well worth imitating in our markedly democratic state." In 1858 Frederick Law Olmsted (1822–1903) together with Calvert Vaux (1824–1895) design New York's "green lung" with walking paths, lakes, quiet areas and open spaces – as a seemingly natural recreational space for people to escape from the rat race of the city. Green spaces are increasingly important in the industrialised and expanding cities: in addition to the aesthetic representative function, the new emphasis is on the social hygienic and democratic function of the public park. Although conceived as landscape parks, the *Tivoli Park* in Copenhagen and the *Prater* in Vienna are transformed however, in part, into amusement parks with shooting-galleries, carousels and pubs. In leisure complexes, such as the *Europa-Park* in Germany's Rust (since 1975) and *Disneyland Paris* (since 1992), the entertainment aspect is more important than the plants, and in the technology theme park *Futuroscope* near Poitiers in France (since 1987), it is the world of technological wonders. The importance of the public parks and city gardens created since industrialisation in the 19th century as recreational and meeting spaces in the middle of large cities should not be underestimated – and that is increasingly true in the 20th and 21st centuries. Whether small green areas such as the community garden, | 2009 URBAN GARDENING III botanical gardens at universities or large "green lungs", such as *Hyde Park* and *Kensington Gardens* in London, *Bois de Boulogne* in Paris, *Tempelhofer Feld* in Berlin, or the *Ueno Park* in Tokyo with its temples: urban green spaces are of existential importance for humans and nature. They provide nesting places for birds, and earth to build dens for foxes, badgers and polecats; they provide stone walls for lizards, fields for crickets, and they house numerous types of plants that are essential for bees and butterflies. A network of green areas in the city maintains and fosters the biodiversity of fauna and flora and also provides humans with easily accessible free spaces to escape their at-times hectic daily lives.

**CIRCA 1850: GARDEN TOOLS AND GARDEN FURNI-
TURE** The 19ᵗʰ century witnesses a boom in the manufacture
of garden tools and furniture. The tools, based on precursors dating
from prehistoric times, such as plant pots, for example, have been
refined by each culture and become increasingly specialised for
specific purposes over the course of centuries, particularly during
the Renaissance.

In the 19ᵗʰ century, spades, hoes, saws, sickles, shears, ladders
and baskets are mass-produced for the first time, complemented by
the manufacture of garden tables and chairs, swings and sunshades.
Gardens have been used as a living room in summer for a very long
time: as far back as the Middle Ages, people sit on *lawn benches,* and
set out wooden chairs and tables or stone tables that remain in the
garden all year long. The 19ᵗʰ century also marks the beginning of the
mass production of cast-iron, wicker or wooden garden furniture, as
well as small pavilions and bowers. The garden lounger and sunshade
become standard features in the 20ᵗʰ century; furniture fashioned
from concrete, Eternit and today primarily plastic is introduced.

1851: GARDEN EXHIBITION II Gardens were first exhibited
at the world's fair in London's *Hyde Park,* the Great Exhibition, in
the *Crystal Palace.* Nowadays, temporary show gardens – which are
set up with a great effort for a few days, where plant varieties, exotic
plants, or new ideas for design are staged – are an important part
of garden architecture and the garden business, whether the Chelsea
Flower Show in London, for which the tickets are purchased already
half a year in advance; the Tatton Park Flower Show and Hampton
Court Flower Show in England; the Bundesgartenschau, the International Garden Exhibition in Dresden, or the State Garden Show in
Bad Oeynhausen/Löhne in Germany; the garden festival Chaumont-
sur-Loire in France; or the Grün 80 and Giardina in Switzerland.

**1859: CULTURAL TRANSFER VI – CHINOISERIE AND
JAPONISM** *Tatton Park* near Manchester is created. It is stunning
not only for its terraces in the Italian style, the large *orangery* and
the beech-lined avenues, but also for its Japanese garden with Shinto

The world's biggest flower show: stand at the Chelsea Flower Show,
London, England

Yearning for the Far East: the Chinese Pagoda in *Kew Gardens*, built in 1762
based on plans by the architect Sir William Chambers (1723–1796),
is nearly 50 metres high. Each storey is 30 cm narrower than the one below it.

temple, which is added in 1910. Chinese or Japanese motifs like those found in *Kew Gardens,* in Munich's *Englische Garten,* in the park at Sanssouci or the tea house and Japanese bridge in the garden at Heale House in Wiltshire in southern England, are en vogue in the 18ᵗʰ and 19ᵗʰ centuries.

Beginning in the 6ᵗʰ century, Japanese garden art also grew from Chinese garden culture, whereby painting and garden design are closely associated: just as the eye follows the landscape depictions along a picture scroll, strollers should make their way from one staged landscape sequence to the next and be surprised by the *views.*

1741 TO 1780: INSPIRATION VII

In Europe, knowledge of Chinese gardens arrived by way of accounts from Marco Polo (circa 1254–1324), and then later – with an enduring effect – the copper engravings by the missionary Matteo Ripa (1682–1746). Ripa, who worked as painter and copper engraver in the court of the Chinese Kangxi Emperor (1654–1722) from 1711 to 1723, influenced European garden design with his copper engravings of the imperial summer palace. As a result, Chinese and Japanese motifs and scenarios are emulated in European gardens as exotic, oriental, small-format cosmos with an artificial lake, hill, and select plants with lanterns, bridges and perhaps pavilions in a corner of a park, or small gardens of moss, stone and water. They are testimony to the great admiration for China's and Japan's philosophically, as well as artistically and religiously, extremely complex art of the garden.

The *Kenroku-en Garden* in Kanazawa, Japan, planted from 1676, which is among the three most important gardens in Japan, is a prototypical example. It fulfils all expectations of the perfect landscape garden as formulated by the ancient Chinese poet Li Gefei in his *Chronicles of the Famous Luoyang Gardens:* circuitousness, seclusion, artistry, tradition, running water and panoramic views are the terms that he names. The park has been on the list of Japan's special places of scenic beauty *(Tokubetsu meishō)* since 1985. Japan has countless gardens of the highest quality in terms of design: in Kyoto alone are the *Kinkaku-ji* with its golden temple (circa 1400), *Ginkaku-ji* with its silver temple (1473), *Ryōan-ji* with its famous stone garden (1450) and *Nanzen-ji* (circa 1620). Gravel, rocks, water, moss and trees – every-

Grandeur and harmony: the Temple of the Golden Pavilion or *Kinkaku-ji*, Kyoto, Japan. The official name of the pavilion, which was built in 1937, is actually *Rokuon-ji* (Deer Garden Temple). In 1994 it was designated a Unesco World Heritage Site.

thing is composed with the utmost care, and walking down the numerous paths is equally restorative, stimulating, refreshing and calming despite the droves of local and international tourists. Those who cannot decode its symbolic language are yet deeply moved by the colours and forms, the clarity and tranquillity.

1867: CONCRETE The French gardener Joseph Monier (1823–1906) takes out a patent on a concrete mix that can be used to manufacture garden vases and plant containers. Employed at first to produce all manner of cast stone designed to resemble anything but concrete, concrete evolves by the mid-20th century into a material for use in the garden that is now accepted in its pure form for path slabs, walls, pergolas and benches. However, terra-cotta is still preferred for pots and containers.

1868: PUBLIC PARKS VI AND RESTORATION II Carl Franz Bally (1821–1899), founder of the Swiss shoe manufactory Bally, begins to drain the swampy land between the River Aare and the railway line Olten–Aarau. At first, Bally has a channel built, which powers the company's own power plant, then an English-style landscape park, which serves as a recreation area for the workforce and the local population. Between 1888 and 1890 the park is expanded: several ponds are added as well as paths on which visitors can explore the park landscape. As is common in English landscape gardens, there is a pavilion, a grotto, a chapel and – as a special feature – a house on stilts. Walking along, one passes from one atmospheric image to the next, discovering viewing axes and the flowers that family members have brought back from their journeys. Untended for decades in the 20th century, *Bally-Park* is restored in the beginning of the 1990s. Meanwhile under historical preservation, it was awarded the Schulthess-Gartenpreis in 2016. | 2006: AWARDS

1876: GLASS HOUSE II In the *Royal Greenhouses in Laeken,* the *Serres Royales de Laeken,* near Brussels, the *Large Winter Garden* is inaugurated. The three-storey dome designed by Alphonse Balat (1818–1895) has a diameter of 57 metres. Ever since the possibility of

Roofed Madagascan rainforest: *Masoala Hall* at Zoo Zurich, Switzerland

architecture made of steel or iron and glass for railway stations and exhibition halls, greenhouses, too, are realised on a palatial scale: the palm houses in *Kew Gardens* are erected as early as 1844–48, while those at the park at Schönbrunn Palace in Vienna, a Unesco World Heritage site, were built in 1879–82. Sir Joseph Paxton (1801–1865) designed not only the gigantic *Crystal Palace;* as chief gardener in Chatsworth, he also built the trendsetting *Large Greenhouse* in 1836–40. Winter gardens are also en vogue for private residences; it is a way of bringing a piece of "nature" into the home or, conversely, extending the living space into the garden. In 2001, the largest palm house to date is completed: the *Eden Project* in Cornwall, where a tropical rainforest is re-created beneath futuristic, transparent domes. *Masoala Rainforest Hall,* based on a concept by the Liechtenstein landscape architect Günther Vogt (*1957) and featuring a Madagascan rainforest, opens at Zoo Zurich in 2003.

1880: ALPINUM II Henri Correvon (1854–1939), a botanist and gardener from Geneva founded, together with comrades, the Association pour la Protection des Plantes; after twenty-five years, the organisation merged with the Schweizerische Naturschutz-bund. The reason: in the second half of the 19th century, botanising develops into such a popular hobby that certain plants soon become threatened. Many English people go "plant hunting" in the Swiss mountains and dig out the plants without any further ado in order to plant them at home in their *alpinums.* Many alpine plants do not survive the change of location and therefore have to be "hunted" again. Around 1880, edelweiss, for example, is threatened with extinction in Switzerland. The most eccentric alpine garden in England is *Friar Park* in Henley-on-Thames, Oxfordshire: in the 1890s, alpine expert Sir Frank Crisp (1843–1919) planted almost 2500 different alpine plants and created a rockery as well as a mini Matterhorn including an ice cave. According to William Robinson, it is the best rock garden of the era. From 1970 *Friar Park* belongs to the Beatles musician George Harrison (1943–2001), who is inspired by the garden to compose, among other songs, the *Ballad of Sir Frankie Crisp (Let It Roll).*

CIRCA 1880: URBAN GARDENING I Urban gardening has been around ever since there have been cities. The more perishable the goods, the more expensive the transport costs, which makes even the smallest plot of cultivable land in a city that much more attractive. In Paris, fruit and vegetables grow on roughly one-sixth of the urban area at the end of the 19th century, and the annual yield is estimated at roughly 100000 tons.

1883: INSPIRATION X The painter Claude Monet (1840–1926) moves to Giverny, roughly seventy kilometres northwest of Paris. He plants his now world-famous (water lily) garden and is able to study the effect of flowers, trees and pond water in different lighting situations without being disturbed. The garden is the inspiration and point of departure for independent scenic pictorial reality in his Late Impressionist water lily paintings. In 2010, German photographer Elger Esser (*1967) devotes a photo series to Monet's garden paradise, a pilgrimage site for tourists for decades and photographed a million times over. Taken by moonlight or at dusk, the *Nocturnes à Giverny* lends the garden new magic again.

Also attesting to the fact that self-grown plants provide the starting material for an artistic encounter are painters such as Max Liebermann (1847–1935), with paintings of his garden at Berlin's Wannsee, and Adolf Dietrich (1877–1957), who in Berlingen in Switzerland constantly turned his gaze to his neighbour's garden. Also the Swiss photographer Thomas Flechtner (*1961) focused on seeds, self-grown flowers and a spice garden in the Cardamom Hills in Kerala, India, for his series *Germs* (2007–2013), *Blumen* (2003–2006) and the 85-part photo series *Spicegarden* (2003), which can be viewed in the patients' rooms of the Universitätsspital Basel. | 2009: GARDEN THERAPY II

1885: MIXED BORDERS, IMPORT IV AND FLOATING GARDEN II The founder of the Madeira Wine Company, John Blandy, bought a property with hunting lodge from the family of the Count of Carvalhal on Madeira and began to plant the *Quinta do Palheiro Ferreiro* garden; it was tended for generations and further developed by Mildred Blandy (1905–1984) and Christina Blandy, in

Garden bed with various perennials selected according to colour and form.
Private garden, England

particular. Under the influence of the gardener and garden journalist William Robinson, the garden is laid out in a "wild style". It captivates through rare plants, such as a Brazilian pine; South African proteas, camellia and rose collections; and the seemingly natural diversity in the arrangement. Robinson's books *The Wild Garden* (1870) and *The English Flower Garden* (1883) popularise the *English cottage garden* and *mixed herbaceous borders:* beds with a variety of perennial plants subtly selected according to colour and design.

The island of Madeira, situated in the middle of the Atlantic on the trade route between Europe, Africa, Asia and America, is called "the floating garden" for good reason; already back then it had long served as (interim) storehouse for exotic plants. In addition to *Quinta do Palheiro Ferreiro,* also *Jardim Botânico da Madeira* above the capital Funchal, planted in 1960 at the former residence of the William Reid family, possesses a variety of exotic plants and an extraordinary cactus garden. Both gardens offer a magnificent view of the capital and the ocean.

1888: GARDENS IN FILM The French inventor and film pioneer Louis Le Prince (1841–1890) shot *Roundhay Garden Scene* with a film camera that he had developed himself. The approximately two-second film fragment, which shows people in a garden in a suburb of Leeds, is considered the oldest preserved sequence in film history. From the gardener comedy *L'Arroseur arrosé* (1895) by the Lumière brothers to Jacques Tati's rockery in *Mon Oncle* (1958) and the crime scene in London's Maryon Park from Michelangelo Antonioni's *Blowup* (1966) through to Joe Wright's screen adaptation of Jane Austen's *Pride & Prejudice* (2005): gardens are not only decorative backgrounds, but also meaningful settings for desires and fears. They represent (paradise) utopias as well as eerie confusion in the thicket of life.

1895: LARGEST GARDEN OWNER Three philanthropic Victorians – the social reformer Octavia Hill (1838–1912), Sir Robert Hunter (1844–1913) and Canon Hardwicke Rawnsley (1851–1920) – found the National Trust for Places of Historic Interest or Natural Beauty in England. They want to protect gardens, buildings and entire land-

Cacti in *Jardim Botânico da Madeira*, Funchal, Portugal

Hestercombe Gardens near Taunton, England, comprise a landscape park laid out in 1750 and a *Victorian terrace* featuring a pergola and orangery designed by Gertrude Jekyll and Sir Edwin Lutyens at the beginning of the 20th century.

scapes from defacement through industrialisation, traffic and building activity. One hundred years later, the National Trust has three million members. It owns 248 000 hectares of landscape worthy of protection in England, Wales and Northern Ireland, 600 miles of coastline, more than 200 historical buildings and important gardens. The National Trust's immense responsibilities are supported not only by patrons, but also by thousands of volunteers who donate their time to work in the cottages, gardens and protected landscapes.

CIRCA 1900: GARDEN CITY The idea of the garden city emerges in Germany and in England around the same time; Sir Ebenezer Howard's (1850–1928) *Garden Cities of Tomorrow* is released in 1898 in London. Neighbourhoods emerge with terraced houses that each have a small garden in front and behind. From 1906, in London, for example, the *Hampstead Garden Suburb* is realised – a particularly beautiful and currently very desirable garden city neighbourhood where the residents decided in 2015 to counteract the use of loud lawnmowers and leaf blowers by using yellow and red penalty cards, like at football games. Healthy lifestyle and self-sufficiency are a key concept, although it fails to function as planned in the garden city Hellerau near Dresden, built in 1907 by the co-founder of the Deutscher Werkbund, Hermann Muthesius (1861–1927), because the workers' homes are too expensive for the working class. Shortly afterwards, Krupp creates a garden settlement for its workers in 1912 on a site in Essen-Margaretenhöhe. At the international art exhibition documenta in Kassel, a low-cost, ecological garden city called *documenta urbana* is realised in 1982. *Parque Güell* in Barcelona is also conceived in the spirit of a garden city. Circa 1900 the architect Antonio Gaudí i Cornet (1852–1926) creates plans for some 60 building lots, a market square and an open-air theatre. In the end, only two lots are developed and the ensemble is embellished with the ornamentally curved walls and colourful ceramic shards so typical of the architect, transforming the site into a cheerful park full of colour.

1904: A SCHOOL FOR GARDENERS Inspired by her interest in the writer John Ruskin, (1819–1900) the architect William Morris

143

At and above the tree-line: wolf's bane, like columbine, campanula and astrantia, thrives in gardens and the wild in the high Alps.

(1834–1896) and the Arts and Crafts Movement, the painter Gertrude Jekyll (1843–1932) embarks on an intense exploration of the art of the garden. Around her house, Munstead Wood in the county of Surrey, southern England, she creates a garden and keeps a photographic journal of the stages of development. She works in close collaboration with the architect Sir Edwin Lutyens (1869–1944) – for example, at Hestercombe, Somerset – and writes fourteen garden books and over 2000 articles, among others for the magazine *The Garden*. It is thanks to her influence, that the first gardeners' school for women is founded in 1904 by Lady Frances Wolseley (1872–1936), the Glynde School for Lady Gardeners, where women can receive professional training as gardeners. The study of garden design at a university is first intro-duced in Berlin in 1929. Along with Jekyll, Ellen Ann Willmott (1858–1934) is also an influential garden designer and author of the book *Warley Garden in Spring and Summer* (1909) and *The Genus Rosa* (1910). She begins designing the garden around her parents' home, Warley Place, and with an inheritance, buys a house close to Aix-les-Bains in France, and in 1905 another near Ventimiglia in Italy. Her passion, however, is the collection and cultivation of plants; she is thought to gather around 100 000 different species. In 1897, she is thus awarded, as the second woman after Jekyll, the Victoria Medal of Honour of the Royal Horticultural Society (RHS), and from 1905 she is among the first women to become a member of the Linnean Society of London. Since she invested all of her wealth in her gardens and plants, she died deeply in debt. Not only have women tended kitchen and flower gardens for millennia; Gertrude Jekyll and Ellen Ann Willmott also mark the start of an illustrious series of influential garden designers and theorists.

1907: ALPINUM III AND GARDEN THERAPY I An alpine garden, first called "alpineum", is planted at the sanatorium for tuber-culosis patients at Davos's Schatzalp in Switzerland. The beauty of edelweiss, bellflowers and other plants is meant to please the patients and support their recovery. In the 1950s, the sanatorium is rebuilt as a hotel and the garden is almost entirely overgrown. However, from 1968 to 1972 it is restored, or rather, redesigned as a botanical garden.

145

Meanwhile added to the Schatzalp forest of spruce, larch, Scots pine and Swiss stone pine are the restored *Alte Alpinum* and the *Neue Alpinum:* roughly 5000 different alpine plants from Switzerland, New Zealand, China, Nepal, Tibet, the Pyrenees and other mountainous regions flourish here, at 1,900 metres above sea level.

Nowadays there are numerous alpine and arctic-alpine gardens, such as the *Jardin Alpin de Meyrin* created in 1880 and the alpine botanical garden *Jardin Flore-Alpe* in Champex-Lac created from 1923 to 1967, both in Switzerland; *Tromsø Arctic-Alpine Botanical Garden* in Norway; *Arctic Alpine Garden Kirovsk* near Murmansk in Russia; *Jardin botanique alpin du Lautaret* in France; and *Giardino Botanico Alpino Saussurea* in Italy.

1909: PUBLIC PARKS VII The *Hamburger Stadtpark* is inaugurated. The garden architect Leberecht Migge (1881–1935) calls for a democratisation of garden art and gardens, saying they should be orientated to the needs of the population for recreation and diversion, as Christian Cay Lorenz Hirschfeld had already conceptualised; social hygiene functions step to the forefront. | 1779 TO 1785: PUBLIC PARKS III A lake created in a basic geometrical shape is surrounded by meadows, a forest and flower beds: Migge, who collaborates with the German architect Bruno Taut (1880–1938) and others, espouses the sensibilities of the Neue Sachlichkeit and the architectural garden and seeks to distance himself from the Romantic landscape park according to the English model, from Victorian garden design with their decorative elements, such as greenhouses, and from Art Nouveau. Resurrecting the geometrical garden is the logical step, which will, however, displace Romantic motifs. At the same time, the idea of the *natural garden* begins to take hold, for example, through the work of Willy Lange (1864–1941), who publishes *Die Gartengestaltung der Neuzeit* in Leipzig (1907). The concept of using indigenous plants anticipates not only nationalistic ideologies but also ecological movements. | FROM 1970: USE AND PLEASURE IV

1911: INSPIRATION XI The children's book *The Secret Garden* by the English-American writer Frances Hodgson Burnett (1849–1924)

is published. A great success as a book, many times adapted for the screen, and in 1991 produced as a musical, the garden from the title is inspired by the overgrown garden of Great Maytham Hall in Kent, England, where Burnett lived from 1889 to 1907. In 1910 the architect Sir Edwin Lutyens renovates the garden.

For Virginia Woolf (1882–1941), too, the garden at her cottage, Monk's House in Rodmell is a site of inspiration for her writing. Woolf's short story *Kew Gardens* is published in 1919. She compares the carpet of flowers in her garden to a cloth: "Our Garden is a perfect variegated chintz: asters, plumasters, zinnias, geums, nasturtiums and so on; all bright, cut from coloured papers, stiff, upstanding as flowers should be." As Rodmell is located close to Sissinghurst Castle, Woolf became acquainted with Vita Sackville-West (1892–1962); the two women were first connected by a love affair and later, a friendship.

1913: AMPHITHEATRE IV Called the *Römische Garten* – or also *Römische Terrasse* – with a view of the Elbe, this was laid out by the businessman Julius Richter (1836–1909) in Hamburg and purchased in 1897 by the German-Jewish banking family Warburg. From 1913, they have the garden extended by their head gardener Else Hoffa (1885–1964): lively summer festivals and theatre performances take place. Hoffa is the first woman in Germany to have a career as a head gardener. After the National Socialist takeover of power, the family, as well as Else Hoffa, are forced to emigrate; the garden declines. In 1951 the Warburgs bequeath the *Römische Garten* to the City of Hamburg. Renovated in the early 1990s, performances again take place in the green setting.

1918: PRIMARY AND SECONDARY COLOURS The manifesto of the artists' association De Stijl is published in the group's magazine of the same name. The painter, designer and magazine publisher Theo van Doesburg (1883–1931) also explores the theme of garden design because he views gardens as a natural extension of the house. For a row-house development in the community of Drachten in the Netherlands (1921) he proposes not only the use of the primary colours blue, red and yellow for doors or window frames, but in

Green amphitheatre: *Römischer Garten* or *Römische Terrasse*,
Hamburg, Germany

particular as a colour scheme in the gardens. When it comes to the agricultural school that is part of the housing development, however, the architect chooses the secondary colours purple, orange and green for stained-glass windows, interiors and geometrically planted garden beds. He designs a vase-like garden sculpture, which he envisions planted with yellow, blue, red and white flowers set on a green lawn. In his representational works, Piet Mondrian (1872–1944), another member of De Stijl, turns to trees and flowers at first, although – or perhaps especially because – nature is said to have stirred and inspired him deeply: thus, on one occasion, he asks his friends Wassily Kandinsky (1866–1944), Hans Arp (1886–1966) and Ben Nicholson (1894–1982) whether they would allow him to sit at a different place at table so that he would not have to look outside. Mondrian's abstract images painted in primary colours, such as *Tableau 1, Composition with Red, Black, Blue and Yellow* (1921) have considerable influence on the design of flower beds in primary colours and geometrical shapes.

CIRCA 1917: URBAN GARDENING II During the First World War, the Canadian Ministry of Agriculture launches a campaign to promote urban vegetable gardening under the title: *A Vegetable Garden for Every Home;* the goal is to supply the population with fresh fruit and vegetables. During the Second World War, *Victory Gardens* or *War Gardens* are again essential for survival: backyards, front gardens, rooftop terraces, football fields and even bomb craters are transformed into vegetable gardens. In the course of the so-called "Anbauschlacht", or crop-growing battle, the Sechseläuten meadow in Zurich becomes a field in 1940. While the small planting activity in Switzerland does not reach the dimensions hoped for in terms of increase in yields, it fulfils its purpose as part of the country's intellectual defence and is therefore supported by all political camps.

Obtaining seeds or seedlings can be difficult in times of war. For that reason, the network *The 15ᵗʰ Garden* arose in Syria: named after 15 March 2011, the beginning of the protests against the government of Bashar al-Assad (*1965). The network connects gardeners in roughly seventeen occupied cities that have been devastated by the war. The goal is the exchange of seeds – donated, among others, from Germany,

France and Sweden and brought into the country through Lebanon – and gardening knowledge. Main crops are cucumbers, tomatoes and aubergines. | 2008: BIODIVERSITY

1923: HANGING GARDENS II The book *Vers une architecture* by the architects Le Corbusier (1887–1965) and Pierre Jeanneret (1896–1967) is published in Paris. Le Corbusier postulates a fundamental right to "sun – air – vegetation", although he assumes that modern men and women live in high-rises and prefer to enjoy gardens like a vista (and like a picture!) in a passive mode. With buildings soaring into the vertical, the gardens of high-rises – and rooftop gardens fitted with plant troughs, like at the Villa Savoye built from 1929 to 1931 in Poissy, France – provide a green area that does not demand too much work.

1924: THEMATIC GARDENS Wilhelmina "Mien" Jacoba Ruys (1904–1999), daughter of a gardener at the Royal Moerheim Nursery in Dedemsvaart, the Netherlands, creates her first garden. Over the course of her life, the progressive garden architect expands Dedemsvaart by adding 25 gardens, among others the water (1954), the herb (1957) and the forest garden (1987). Her first garden, the *overgrown garden* (1924), is laid out beneath apple trees and around a square pool (renovated in 2001). The *old testing garden* – a garden of herbaceous perennials and shrubs designed in the English manner with a concrete slab path that inspired Ruys to develop the Grion stone, a precursor of exposed aggregate concrete slabs – has also gained fame.

1927/28: LOVE OF GEOMETRY III In the French town of Hyères, a sensational, geometric garden is established at the Villa Noailles. The design of Gabriel Guévrékian (1900–1970) and Robert Mallett-Stevens (1886–1945) is based on Guévrékian's idea from 1925, when he proposes a triangular garden with triangular flower beds as borders for tetrahedron structures of coloured glass. The garden of the Villa Noailles takes the form of a giant, triangular box divided into rectangular and triangular modules of equal size. Depending on

Rooftop garden with pictorial character: Le Corbusier's Villa Savoye, built between 1929 and 1931, has been a Unesco World Heritage Site since 2016.

the season, a variety of plants such as box or aloe in a bed of gravel are cultivated in each module or plant container.

1930: GARDENS BY COLOUR The writer and gardener Vita Sackville-West (1892–1962) begins to transform the dilapidated castle and the "desert of stinging nettles" at Sissinghurst Castle in Kent in southern England, into a now world-famous garden. *The White Garden,* a garden space planted in 1948, in which among others, white roses, clematis, wisteria, cosmos and white honeysuckle create a minimalist and entirely romantic atmosphere, is visited, or rather infested annually by thousands of tourists as a paradisiacal place of longing. *Sissinghurst* can be cited as one of the most influential gardens of the 20th century along with Captain Lawrence Johnston's (1871–1958) *Hidcote Manor Garden,* an Arts-and-Crafts garden in the county of Gloucestershire: the idea of designing gardens by colour is emulated around the world. Sackville-West's gardening column in the *Observer* becomes a cult feature among readers and has a decisive influence on garden design.

1935: STAGED NATURE The *Hohle Gasse* in Küssnacht am Rigi, Switzerland where – according to Schiller – Wilhelm Tell killed the tyrannical Landvogt (or governor) Gessler with a bow and arrow, happens to be restored shortly before the outbreak of war: to save this legendary site harking back to the founding days of the Swiss Confederation, a bypass is built and the tree-lined sunken path between erratic blocks is transformed into a significant landscape in the style of a landscape park.

1941/42: BREAK During the Second World War, in most European countries, many gardens and parks were heavily damaged. In spared Switzerland, on the contrary, a garden is able to be created in the midst of the war – and perhaps significantly – on the grounds of the weapons manufacturer Waffen- und Werkzeugmaschinenfabrik Bührle in Zurich-Oerlikon. Designed by Swiss landscape architect Gustav Ammann (1885–1955) and used by the personnel as a small recreational space, the park seems more like a private garden than a

Structuring garden spaces with colours: *The White Garden* in Vita Sackville-West's park at Sissinghurst Castle, Cranbrook, Kent, England

Garden in the spirit of the Swiss National Exhibition of 1939:
Gustav-Ammann-Park, Zurich, Switzerland

public park. It goes without saying that the war era creates a hiatus in the realisation of public gardens and parks, and many work biographies of landscape architects show a gap during this period. One exception is the Italian garden architect Maria Teresa Parpagliolo Shepard (1903–1974), who works on the E42 World's Fair planned by Benito Mussolini in Rome and designs monumental garden ensembles in the Classicist vein between 1938 and 1942. Parpagliolo, opportunistic and with little consideration for the politics of the time, is interested in contemporary German garden design although she prefers indigenous Italian plant species and is thus very much in step with the nationalistic Fascist (garden-) culture. After the war, she makes her home in England, where she is able to quickly establish a name for herself, working – among others – with Sylvia Crowe (1901–1997), one of the most important English landscape architects in post-war England. Crowe made a name for herself with the planning of New Towns, entirely newly designed settlements; her book *Garden Design*, published in 1958, had a decisive influence on garden design. As cities are being reconstructed, landscape architecture flourishes as well: the surroundings of new residential developments, hospitals, schools, factories or office buildings are transformed into green spaces; gardens and parks are restored. Indeed, the creation of new gardens is widely regarded as part of the universal cultural renewal. "The most recent tradition in the history of gardens is even now being formulated in America (...)", writes Sylvia Crowe. "It reveals a distant kinship with the English landscape garden and is informed in the use of plants by the styles of William Robinson and Gertrude Jekyll. A strong Japanese influence is noticeable, although the tendency toward a new and free use of the form must be seen as springing from the influence of the Bauhaus."

1947: 1001 ARABIAN NIGHTS II The French painter Jacques Majorelle (1886–1962) makes *Jardin Majorelle* in Marrakesh accessible to the public; an inheritance from his father, who died in 1926, had made it possible for him to build his villa and the garden. *Jardin Majorelle* is a botanical garden with plants from all five continents, mainly cacti and bougainvillea. In 1980 the meanwhile overgrown gar-

Green lung: *Parque do Ibirapuera,* São Paulo, Brazil

den is purchased and restored by fashion designer Yves Saint Laurent (1936–2008) and his life- and business partner Pierre Bergé (*1930). Today, the garden in the centre of Marrakesh – the final resting place of Yves Saint Laurent – attracts thousands of tourists from around the world every year.

FROM 1950: GARDENERS, GARDEN MUSEUMS The professional title of garden designer gradually shifts into that of garden or landscape architect. The professional profile of the gardener – as someone who works in the garden and possesses botanical as well as aesthetic and practical skills – was originally defined during the rediscovery of the garden culture in the Renaissance, after which it was gradually differentiated into three professional groups: garden designer, botanist and gardener, with the expansion of plant research. Despite his hard work exposed to wind and all kinds of weather, the gardener is often envied for closeness to nature; in literature, he is portrayed as an odd good-for-nothing (Eichendorff's *Taugenichts*), a seducer (Lawrence's *Lady Chatterley*) and sometimes the dirty old man and (not) always the murderer. In the 17th-century garden, design enjoyed equal status with the other arts; today it is a part of landscape architecture. In the year 2000, a museum for garden art is opened at Fantaisie Castle in Bayreuth, followed in 2002 by the Benrath Palace and Park Foundation, Düsseldorf.

1953: LOVE OF GEOMETRY IV Among many other projects, the Finnish architect, designer, garden designer and artist Alvar Aalto (1898–1976) realises a rigorously geometrical garden at his home Villa Mairea in the Finnish town of Noormarkku, in which the stylisation and parallels between architectonic and botanical forms are a key component. Aalto's influence on European, and in particular on Scandinavian garden design is significant.

1954: PUBLIC PARKS VII *Parque do Ibirapuera* opens in São Paulo. Designed by the Brazilian landscape architects Roberto Burle Marx (1909–1994) and Otávio Teixeira Mendes (1907–1988), the city garden's importance for the population is comparable with that of New York's *Central Park*. Although self-taught as a landscape architect, the painter and plant connoisseur Roberto Burle Marx is considered one of the most important garden designers ever. He provided crucial impulses to garden design with his curve- and wave-shaped plantings of lush Brazilian flora. As congenial partner of the architects Lucio Costa (1902–1998), Le Corbusier and Oscar Niemeyer (1907–2012), he designed numerous squares, gardens and parks, such as *Praça de Casa Forte* in Recife (1937), the gardens of the public buildings in the capital Brasilia (1965), and the 4-kilometre-long beach promenade on the Copacabana in Rio de Janeiro (1970). From 1949, south of Rio de Janeiro Burle Marx operated *Sítio Santo Antônio da Bica*, a nursery where he cultivated tropical plants for use in gardens; in 1985 he bequeathed the site to the state.

FROM 1960: LAND ART AND INSPIRATION XII The Swiss garden architect Ernst Cramer (1898–1980) opens a window onto an international horizon with his *Poet's Garden,* realised in 1959 for the First Swiss Garden Exhibition G59: with its restrained formal language and plant selection, the poetic garden sets a style trend and is featured in the 1964 publication on pioneers of Land Art released by the Museum of Modern Art in New York. Land Art – Robert Smithson (1938–1973), Walter de Maria (1935–2013) and Richard Long (*1945) are important protagonists – aims to create the prerequisites for experiences in perception, whereby the artworks do not utilise the landscape as a backdrop but become landscape in their own right: the given landscape and the artistic intervention converge into a new unified whole. Land- or Earth-Art works change as a result of exposure to the elements, they erode, wash out or melt (if they are made of snow and ice); plans, sketches, photographs or films document the individual projects. The Land and Minimal Art movements and the new ecological awareness bring about a rapprochement between art and garden architecture. Plantings regarded as works of art change in form, grow and are transformed in appearance according to season, and parks and gardens are designed in a formal language inspired by Minimal Art.

Cool poetry: Ernst Cramer's *Poet's Garden* at the G59 Garden Exhibition,
Zurich, Switzerland

1961: SCULPTURE PARK I *Otterlo-Park* near Arnhem, Holland is opened to the public. The park, created by Dutch landscape architect Jan Bijhouwer (1898–1974) for the art collector couple Helene and Anton Kröller-Müller around their museum opened in 1938 containing works by Vincent van Gogh (1853–1890), is an open-air museum for around 160 sculptures by Henry Moore (1898–1986), Jean Dubuffet (1901–1985), Marta Pan (1923–2008) and other artists. At the same time, *Otterlo-Park* is part of the larger *Nationaal Park de Hoge Veluwe*, where Helene Kröller-Müller (1869–1939) had had sculptures placed from 1915. Sculpture exhibitions in London's *Battersea Park* and *Park Sonsbeek* near Arnhem inspired her to establish her own sculpture park.

1961–1965: MODERNISM IN ITALY Pietro Porcinai (1910–1986) creates one of his most outstanding gardens at the Villa Il Roseto in Florence. Porcinai is among those Italian garden architects who contributed to the renewal of the garden culture so rich in tradition. Fascinated by the Renaissance and inspired by socialist ideals, he begins from 1931 onwards to design a series of gardens. In creating gardens, he has a preference for squares and rectangles, circular motifs, patterns of intertwining paths and geometrically pruned plants instead of built elements. His list of commissions comprises a total of 1318 garden projects, of which numerous are unfortunately no longer extant.

1963: MODERNISM IN ENGLAND The Danish architect, designer and garden designer Arne Jacobsen (1902–1971) is commissioned to create a new extension for St. Catherine's College at Oxford. A passionate gardener himself, he designs not only the new buildings, interiors and furniture, but also the garden. The college is a gesamtkunstwerk of architecture and garden design, which has given Oxford a modern spirit without breaking with tradition. A circular lawn with an asymmetrically planted cedar forms the centre of the college; there is a canal and the rectangular wall and hedge panels are a characteristic design element. In 1965, rare species are added to the plantings, which Jacobsen is said to have judged as too lush.

A place for rest and recreation: garden designed by the Danish architect
Arne Jacobsen, St. Catherine's College, Oxford, England

20ᵗʰ-century *sunken garden:* sunken grave lots in *Eichbühl cemetery,*
Zurich, Switzerland

1966: TOMB GARDENS V *Eichbühl cemetery* in Zurich is an outstanding project realised by the Swiss landscape architect Fred Eicher (1927–2010), who designed, among others, the *Botanical Garden Zurich* (1977) and the garden of the Swiss Embassy in Brasilia (1982). The cemetery is stunning in its simplicity and expansiveness, the structuring concrete elements and terraced or sunken grave lots. The design of cemeteries or tombs is very much determined by religion, culture, as well as the climate and social change: while crosses and tombstones are still surrounded by lawns in English *lawn cemeteries* and rarely decorated with flowers, gravel and marble or stone slabs are common in Italy where the grave is frequently decorated with plastic flowers and a photographic portrait of the deceased. World-famous cemeteries are the Zentralfriedhof in Vienna or the Père Lachaise in Paris, where many famous artists have been interred. Designed originally by Théodore Brongniart (1739–1813) with cypress, poplar and willow trees as a landscape park and elysion in the spirit of Rousseau, the Père Lachaise is soon popular among prominent figures and the wealthy, and its original form is barely visible. In Switzerland, most graves are today tended by cemetery gardeners, who decorate all graves with the same flowers for the sake of simplicity, changing the plantings only according to season. The uniformity of the rows of graves cannot be explained by rational and cost-efficient grave management alone; it also corresponds to the uniformity of tidy gardens around single-family homes and housing developments. *Kannenfeldpark* in Basel, on the contrary, a cemetery until the 1940s, has become a popular public park with its lawns and collection of various species of trees.

FROM 1968: GARDEN TIPS V The now legendary BBC television show *Gardeners' World* is broadcast for the first time. Transmitted until 2003 from the garden of the current host, shows on garden practice are still being broadcast today, offering random tips, so to speak, for design and planting. Many other shows, too, provide contributions to garden history and landscape architecture, and present famous parks, gardens and landscape architects. From 2000, TV programmes have increasing competition from the Internet, while innumerable garden blogs focus on everything imaginable related to the care and upkeep, design and history of gardens.

FROM 1970: USE AND PLEASURE IV The characteristics of urban, industrial, agrarian and natural landscapes are being discussed. Insight into ecology and the new environmental awareness are increasingly influential with regard to the design of gardens, public squares and landscapes. Landscape architecture begins to focus on the design of all types of open spaces: squares in cities or green spaces along highways are themes as significant as the classic garden architects' tasks for single-family homes, schools or parks. The debate surrounding the *natural-garden* concept with indigenous plants and organic cultivation reaches its apotheosis at the Second Swiss Garden Exhibition "Grün 80".

1977: SCULPTURE PARK II Peter Murray, docent for art education, founded *Yorkshire Sculpture Park* in Wakefield; England's first sculpture park. Honoured as Museum of the Year in 2014, the park meanwhile attracts around 350 000 visitors per year. Situated on open meadows and in small groups of trees are works by Henry Moore, Dame Barbara Hepworth (1903–1975), Andy Goldsworthy (*1956), Sol LeWitt (1928–2007), James Turrell (*1943) and other contemporary artists, and also those affiliated with Land Art.

FROM 1979: AMPHITHEATRE V A generous amphitheatre covered with grass is added to the garden of the Aarhus University designed by Danish landscape architect Carl Theodor Sørensen (1893–1979) and further developed after his death by C.F. Møller Architects; the amphitheatre is the site's visual and social centre.

FROM 1980: INSTANT GARDEN The American garden architect Martha Schwartz (*1950) demonstrates that gardens are artificially created natural environments that also thematicise the artificiality of our world. Together with Peter Walker (*1932), she realises numerous projects in the United States; in Germany her work is represented at the airport garden (1995) and the Swiss Re offices

Artificial garden: rooftop garden at the Whitehead Institute for Biomedical Research, Cambridge, MA, U.S., designed by the garden architect Martha Schwartz

in Munich (2002). Her most uncompromising garden is undoubtedly
the roof garden at the Whitehead Institute for Biomedical Research,
in Cambridge, Massachusetts, U.S., with synthetic *topiary*. Schwartz
comments: "For this commission they all wanted something green
and wanted it fast." Since the roof cannot support planting, and since
there is neither water nor money for maintaining greenery, she
constructs an artificial garden: "Therefore, this work is all about the
idea of the garden per se and the expectation [we have] of a garden –
this mantra, that everything must be fast, cheap and green. (...) This
garden was an angry response to these attitudes. It said: if you want
green and don't want to pay, there, take this!" Plastic it would be!
Aquarium gravel tinted green, green walls and pruned hedges of artificial turf stretched over rolled steel, which serve as benches, create
a green oasis replete with quotations on the roof of the building –
topiary, medieval *lawn benches* and Japanese garden art exist cheek by
jowl. The garden requires no time and no tending to grow: it is the
instant garden par excellence. After 2000, *Instant Gardening* appeared
as a popular trend: there was a sharp increase in sales of evergreen
potted plants with which one can immediately green terraces.

1982: SCULPTURE PARK III The art collector Karl-Heinrich
Müller (1936–2007) purchases the villa and the overgrown English
landscape park at Hombroich, Germany. He commissions the landscape architect Bernhard Korte (*1942) to transform the landscape
with water meadows into a sculpture garden featuring chiefly works
from classic Modernism and contemporary art. In 1994 the grounds
are significantly expanded through the acquisition of the nearby
rocket station; the former hangars and bunkers of the military base
are converted into living and studio spaces for artists and serve as
event venues for lectures or concerts.

1983: NATURAL GARDEN After Atelier Stern & Partner/
Gerwin Engel (*1943) and Eduard Neuenschwander (1924–2013) win
the design competition for *Irchelpark* near the University of Zurich,
the earthworks begin. Rooted in the environmental movement of
the 1970s, *Irchelpark* is an icon of the natural garden movement in

Forest garden and meadowland as exhibition space:
sculptures by the German sculptor Anatol Herzfeld (*1931) on the Museum Insel Hombroich,
Neuss, Germany

Naturalistic landscape park with lake:
the *Irchelpark* near the University of Zurich, Switzerland

Switzerland: a naturalistic landscape with meadows, woods and marshes, as well as an artificial lake are staged in urban surroundings university, residential area and highway feeder roads. There are no beds with colourful and quickly growing flowers, but instead, local wild hedges and, for example, maple, pine, birch, willow and oak trees. Stairs of stone blocks and plants lead to the university campus, artworks by Swiss sculptors make the site a sculpture park too; and tennis courts and a jogging path turn it into a sports park. The park, which was incomplete and sparse at the start, has meanwhile developed to become an important urban recreational and meeting space.

1986: POST-MODERNISM IN FRANCE In creating the *Parc de la Villette* in Paris, the Swiss architect Bernard Tschumi (*1944) realises a multipurpose park on the site of a former abattoir; at roughly 35 hectares, it is the second largest park in Paris. The former Grande Halle accommodates a restaurant and a hall for cultural events; the complex includes a museum of music, a cinema in a futuristic, sphere-shaped building called La Géode, alternating theme gardens linked by paths paved in blue, red metal sculptures dotted at regular intervals throughout the grounds and based on Jacques Derrida's (1930–2004) philosophy of deconstruction, as well as large lawns for sports and games. In short: this Post-Modern park unifies a wide variety of interests and needs, all the while making the stage-like quality and artificiality of "nature" evident at all times.

1988: STROLLING The Swiss sociologist Lucius Burckhardt (1925–2003) gives a lecture on research on walks at the Polytechnic Kassel. The so-called "promenadology" focuses on forgotten, nondescript sites or landscapes burdened with a negative image. Since there is virtually no untouched nature left in all of Central Europe – that is, since the landscape is more or less designed and shaped and can be viewed as a large garden – question of what constitutes a garden has also become a question of perception. The boundary of where a garden begins and where the landscape ends has become blurred. Gardens exist not only outside, but also on rooftops, terraces, balconies and indoors in company buildings or airport terminals. They

A place to gather one's thoughts and reflect: garden at the Swiss Re Centre for Global Dialogue, designed by Dieter Kienast, Rüschlikon, Switzerland

climb from floor to floor in the form of *vertical gardens* and create oases for employees and travellers. | 1994: HANGING GARDENS III The Swiss garden architect Dieter Kienast (1945–1998), who stirred a furore with his garden at the festival of gardens in Chaumont-sur-Loire in 1996, is also interested in the topic of perception. Kienast determines the potentials inherent in a site and emphasises them with minimal means: paths, walls, canals and pools structure the site in a sensitive and precise manner. He cites the artist Robert Morris (*1931), a proponent of Minimal Art: "Simplicity of form should not be equated with simplicity of experience." In preparing the basic concept of a garden, he also studies traces inscribed into the site by both history and garden history. Kienast incorporates lettering – for example, fashioned from concrete – into the design; part word, part sculpture, they charge the garden with several layers of meaning.

1990: CACTUS GARDEN The artist César Manrique (1919–1992) created the *Jardín de cactus* in a former quarry near Guatiza on the island of Lanzarote. Extremely diverse local cacti grow on the bottom of the hollow and the terraced slopes of the quarry. The black volcanic soil sets the stage for the various hues of green and forms of the succulents. It is actually a *sunken garden*, in which the cacti are protected from the sometimes severe winds.

FROM 1990: REVITALISATION Industrial wastelands, former mining regions and urban voids between housing developments and highways are redesigned by landscape architects: thus Michel Desvigne (*1958) and Christine Dalnoky (*1956) plant small birch forests between the houses in a Paris housing development, and on the urban edge of Montpellier they create a "landscape that lasts two minutes" by planting pines along the highway.

In the landscape park *Duisburg-Nord,* designed by Peter Latz (Latz & Partner), or in the Lausitz near Leipzig, abandoned coal mining regions have been revitalised through reforestation and garden design, which is very much inspired by Land and Minimal Art. The *Parc André Citroën* in Paris – realised from 1988 to 1992 by Gilles Clément (*1943) and Alain Provost (1930–2002) on the site of a former

Terraced slopes in a former quarry: the *Jardín de cactus* by the artist César Manrique, Guatiza, Lanzarote, Spain

car factory – is a playful reprisal of stylistic traditions in other Parisian gardens with obliquely arranged, rectangular lawns, a white and a *blue garden* and a square where children can run through water fountains. Architectural elements, water features and plants merge into an ensemble notable for its rationality and poetry, severity and wit.

Finally, in the converted and renovated docklands of London's Canary Wharf, the Belgian landscape architect Jacques Wirtz (*1924) creates the *Jubilee Park* (2002–2004); more specifically, this park is a roof garden above the Jubilee Line Underground station. Wirtz, who collaborates with his sons Martin and Peter from 1990 onwards, is also a passionate gardener in his private life. His gardens are distinguished by an organic formal language with beech, yew or box pruned into shapes: thus a cloud-shaped hedge, inspired by Japanese garden art, invests the *Schoten* garden in Belgium with an abstract modern and yet fairy-tale-like atmosphere. Wirtz's *Jardin du Carrousel* between the *Jardin des Tuileries* and the Louvre in Paris or the impressive water cascades with fountain in the park at Alnwick Castle in Northumberland, England, are stylistically formative for the contemporary landscape architecture.

1993: HORTUS CONCLUSUS III AND SCIENCE IV

The garden of the Fondation Louis Jeantet in Geneva is designed as a *hortus conclusus*: at night, when it is illuminated, as well as by day and especially in spring, when the scarlet cherry trees erupt into pink blossoms, this courtyard garden stands as a modern, poetic version of the paradise garden of old. The Paris firm Agence Ter – founded in 1986 by Henri Bava (*1957), Michel Hoessler (*1958) and Olivier Philippe (*1954) – designs the *Monbijou-Park* in Berlin (1993), gardens for the International Garden Exhibition in Dresden (1995) and the Landesgartenschau (State Garden Show) Bad Oeynhausen/Löhne (1997), and designs an unusually generous, geometrically structured garden ensemble for the Lycée Philippe Lamour in Nîmes, which does more than simply provide some greenery for the school building: it makes the school into a place *within* the garden.

Begun in the late 1970s, the roughly 120-hectare *Garden of Cosmic Speculation* in Scotland's Portrack by Charles Jencks (*1939) and his

Repurposing: *Parc André Citroën* by Gilles Clément and Alain Provost
on the former site of a car factory, Paris, France

Urban green: *Jubilee Park* by Jacques Wirtz on the roof of an Underground railway station on the Jubilee Line, London, England

wife Maggie Keswick (?–1995) has grown into one of the most spectacular landscape parks in Europe. Inspired, among other things, by Land Art, the earth formations and lakes visualise above all discoveries in the natural sciences, such as chaos theory and cosmology, Chinese garden culture and geomancy, which Maggie Keswick occupied in depth. The vegetable garden, for example, is dedicated to the human DNA and the six senses; sculptures symbolise the theories and the senses.

1994: HANGING GARDENS III

French garden architect and tropical forest specialist Patrick Blanc (*1953) presented his *Mur Végétal* at the annual garden festival Chaumont-sur-Loire. *Vertical gardens* or *botanical bricks* are based on an invention by the American professor for landscape architecture Stanley Hart White (1891–1979). Blanc perfected the process both technically and botanically. On research expeditions through forests in Thailand, Peru, Borneo and Australia, he gathered inspiration for his, at times, spectacular projects, such as the greened walls of the Hotel Pershing Hall in Paris (2001) and those of Caixa Forum in Madrid (2008) built by Herzog & de Meuron or for the garden on Jean Nouvel's (*1945) high-rise *One Central Park* in Sydney (2013). *Botanical bricks* act as biofilters against air pollution in cities. This has led to an increase in high-rises planted with vegetation in Chinese metropolises, which are particularly affected by smog.

1996: THE GARDEN AS GARDEN HISTORY

The *Jardins de l'imaginaire,* designed by the American landscape architect Kathryn Gustafson (*1951) for the French town of Terrasson-Lavilledieu in the Périgord, is opened to the public. The park, which covers an area of 6 hectares, is a garden of the history of gardens. The sponsors had originally envisioned a park that was to combine the Italian Renaissance with French Baroque and Japanese meditation culture. But Gustafson goes beyond citing individual historical motifs; instead, she rethinks them and connects them into a harmonious whole, in which watercourses, water jets and fountains constitute the linking elements. Thus water flows over a flight of steps in the *Fôret des jets,* where

Construction of Elysian landscapes: slip road *Sortie Conthey (VS)*, 2002, from the series *Paysage A* by the Swiss photographer Nicolas Faure (*1949)

Translating scientific knowledge into a park: the *Garden of Cosmic Speculation* by Charles Jencks and Maggie Keswick, Portrack, Scotland

Wandering through the history of gardens: the *Jardins de l'imaginaire*
by Kathryn Gustafson, Terrasson-Lavilledieu, France

Nature and art: *Planet der Schweine* (2001) by the German artist Peter Nagel (*1963) and, in the background, *Soglio* (1994) by the English sculptor Nigel Hall (*1943), *Schönthal Abbey Sculpture Park*, Langenbruck, Switzerland

a forest of water jets shoots up into the sky – a reinterpretation of water features in Renaissance gardens. There are five fountains, representing the five major rivers of the world – the Euphrates, Nile, Ganges, Mississippi and Amazon – lined up along the path that bisects the *bois sacré;* they serve as reminders of the vital importance of water for every garden and life in general and of the origins of the history of gardens in Mesopotamia. The *Diana, Princess of Wales Memorial Fountain* which opens in 2004 in London's *Hyde Park* is also designed by Kathryn Gustafson.

FROM 1995: AMPHITHEATRE VI The park at Heveningham Hall, Suffolk, designed by Lancelot "Capability" Brown shortly before his death in 1783, is restored by the English landscape architect Kim Wilkie (*1956) and partially reinterpreted. He replaces the *Victorian Garden* near the house with a grass-covered terrace that runs in a semicircle around the house, thus making it the main character on the stage of the garden.

2000: SCULPTURE PARK IV After a varied history, *Schönthal Abbey* near Langenbruck in Switzerland, first mentioned in 1145, becomes an exhibition site through the art collector John Schmid (*1937), and the vegetable garden near the church and the surrounding landscape are made into a sculpture park. Since the very beginnings of garden history, sculptures have been exhibited in gardens. But whereas in the 19th century, sculptures of important artists or national heroes were exhibited in the parks, in the course of the 20th century, gardens become established as important, also temporary venues for exhibitions of contemporary sculpture – for instance, the annual *Skulptur Projekte Münster* or the exhibitions in the framework of the documenta in Kassel, Germany. *Schönthal Abbey* Sculpture Park is meanwhile an especially fine example of the dialogue of art, garden culture and nature. Strolling along the entwined paths winding through the former monastery complex and park, one successively discovers works by Ian Hamilton Finlay (1925–2006), Roman Signer, Martin Disler (1949–1996), Gerda Steiner (*1967) and Jörg Lenzlinger (*1964), Erik Steinbrecher (*1963) and Miriam Cahn (*1949).

2000: HANGING GARDENS IV At the EXPO in Hanover, the Dutch architecture firm MVRDV (Winy Maas, Jacob van Rijs, Nathalie de Vries) presents a new version of the *Hanging Gardens* in the shape of their spectacular pavilion. Under the heading New Nature, the architects turn their minds to the idea of reclaiming land in the vertical plane: the pavilion is a stacked landscape, a "multi-level park" in which the feasibility of nature is a central motif. From the top down there is first a waterscape with windmills, a multimedia theatre broadcasting information on the Netherlands, one level below visitors already walk through real trees ... forest and, yet another floor down, they find themselves in the "root layer", where the infrastructure of the country is transformed into a theme. Next is a floor on the theme of land reclaimed from the sea and transformed into fertile agricultural land, and at the very bottom a landscape of dunes. The entire pavilion is set into a flower garden.

FROM 2000: URBAN GREEN Nature's potential and purpose in the city is newly discussed under terms such as "urban nature", "urban green", "guerrilla gardening", "urban gardening", and "urban farming". The environmental movement active since the 1970s sees urban and community gardens as more than an alternative green world to the concrete grey. With *Guerrilla Gardening* – for example, secretly spreading mallow seeds – inhabitants appropriate unused interstitial spaces, beautify their cities, or design meeting places and sites where people can become socially and politically involved. The astonishing capacity for renewal of both flora and fauna is demonstrated in industrial wastelands or abandoned railway lands such as the *Schöneberger Südgelände* (southern railway yards) in Berlin, where a biotope was created and where today numerous animal and plant species are found that had disappeared in previous years. Meanwhile, *urban gardening* and *urban farming* as well as the eco-physiology of the plants in urban surroundings are studied and taught at universities. Since most large parks in city centres date at the very latest from the 19th century, new parks and large gardens are more likely to be created on the periphery, in new districts or – if in the city centre – on the occasion of new developments or renovation projects. In London, for

Multi-level park: the Dutch pavilion at the Expo 2000
in Hanover, Germany

Large-format arbour: *MFO-Park* in Oerlikon, Zurich, Switzerland

example, a former power plant is converted into the Tate Gallery of Modern Art; the garden ensemble is the work of Günther Vogt (Vogt Landscape Architects). Vogt, who began by collaborating with Dieter Kienast, creates a relatively small yet clearly structured and poetic garden with far-reaching impact around the massive building on the riverbank of the Thames, complete with small birch forests and lawns. The garden seems to embody Le Corbusier's dictum of "sun – air – vegetation" | 1923: HANGING GARDENS II in the heart of the city, the garden sets the mood for visiting an exhibition by virtue of its meditative tranquillity and clarity. Vogt also collaborates with the architects Herzog & de Meuron on projects for the Laban Centre for Contemporary Dance in London, where he composes stairs from grass fields, and the surroundings of the football stadium Allianz Arena in Munich.

2001–2004: ALPINE GARDENS

The architects Miller & Maranta renovate Villa Garbald, built by architect Gottfried Semper (1803–1879) in Castasegna, Switzerland, and expanded with a tower-like secondary building to become a seminar centre of the Swiss Federal Institute of Technology (ETH). The landscape architect and garden historian Jane Sarah Bihr-de Salis restores the meanwhile overgrown garden designed by Semper. Hydrangeas camellias, false cypresses, hollies, ivy, grapes and roses as well as apricot trees make this small garden in the southern Alps a site of power, contemplation and recreation. Bihr-de Salis has designed, restored, tended and planted several historical gardens in alpine surroundings since 1986, such as the garden of the Hotel Palazzo Salis in Soglio and of the Palazzo Salis in Bondo in Switzerland. In addition, she developed the garden concept for the architect Peter Zumthor's home in Haldenstein.

2002: ARBOUR

MFO-Park is opened in the Oerlikon district of Zurich. On the grounds of the former Maschinenfabrik Oerlikon, the architects Burckhardt + Partner erect a metal trellis – 100 metres long, 35 metres wide and 17 metres high – which is planted with greenery by Raderschallpartner landscape architects. Furnished with climbing supports, planting bowls, stairs, pergolas and balconies, it is a huge

185

Southern alpine climate: garden of the Palazzo Salis in Soglio, Switzerland,
which, together with the garden of the Palazzo Salis in Bondo,
won the 2009 Schulthess-Gartenpreis.

arbour, overgrown with various climbing plants, such as wisteria, honeysuckle and wild vines. *MFO-Park* – a contemporary-romantic meeting point and a venue for cultural events – was honoured in 2010 with the European Garden Prize of the European Garden Heritage Network. Arbours, first popular in England in the 18ᵗʰ century as protected places for sitting and reading, quickly became fashionable throughout the world and are featured in 1853 giving their name (Laube) to the first illustrated mass media in German, the magazine published from 1853 to 1944, *Die Gartenlaube – illustrirtes Familienblatt*.

2003: RESTORATION III On 26 December, an earthquake destroys the city of Bam in central Iran, which had been declared a Unesco World Heritage site. Tens of thousands perish. Because the more than 800-year-old irrigation system of the oasis has been buried by the earthquake, thousands of date palms, pomegranate trees and vines also suffer from acute water shortage. Experts in Afghanistan mend the *qanats:* like hundreds of years ago, | AFTER 750 BC: LANDSCAPE PARK I holes and connecting tunnels are dug at regular intervals; the bottom of each of the holes must lie on the same plane with a gradual drop. Today, water collected in the mountains some 45 km in the distance once again flows through the oasis of Bam.

2003: USE AND PLEASURE V In the framework of the World Horticultural Exhibition (IGA) in Rostock, a symposium takes place entitled *Die grüne Stadt* (the green city). A foundation with the same name was created in order to support and further interdisciplinary debate and research on the ecological, social, health and economic use of green spaces. *Die grüne Stadt,* for example, demonstrates the benefit of a one-hundred-year-old deciduous tree: with a 12-m-wide treetop, one can estimate around 600 000 leaves that absorb around eighteen kilograms of carbon dioxide on a sunny day, and produce around 13 kilograms of oxygen, which covers the oxygen needs of roughly ten people.

2005: ARTISTS' GARDENS AND ARTIFICIAL MOUN-TAIN III The garden created by the Swiss artist Katja Schenker (*1968) is inaugurated in the courtyard of the Federal Institute for

National Topography in Berne, Switzerland. A three-dimensional asphalt map torn, so to speak, into pieces is laid out in the courtyard of the complex. Box, which has become a traditional sculptural element since the art of *topiary* was first established, grows out of the fissures and holes in the map. Artists' gardens in the true sense are *Perry Green* by Henry Moore (1898–1986) in Hertfordshire in the south of England, Niki de Saint Phalle's (1930–2002) *Giardino dei Tarocchi* south of Grosseto in Italy, *Il Gardino di Daniel Spoerri* (*1930) in Tuscany, Ian Hamilton Finlay's *Little Sparta* in Stonypath near Edinburgh or Derek Jarman's (1942–1994) *Prospect Cottage* garden in Dungeness on England's south coast. Jarman creates it when terminally ill and calls it "therapy and medicine", declaring, "Paradise haunts gardens, and some gardens are paradises. Mine is one of them." Also noteworthy are *Barbara Hepworth Sculpture Garden* in Cornwall and Constantin Brâncuşi's (1876–1957) sculpture garden *Târgu Jiu* near Hobitza in Romania. They are all – entirely different – examples of gardens by artists in which the creator's understanding of art and nature is melded to a unique unity.

The Danish artist Olafur Eliasson (*1967), whose work deals with the borders and overlaps of art, nature, culture and science, realises several garden artworks: together with the landscape architect Günther Vogt, in 2001 he creates a sequence of spaces *The Mediated Motion,* at the Kunsthaus Bregenz, by means of which visitors can reflect on simulated nature, and in 2016 in the palace and park of Versailles, he creates several installations – including a huge waterfall sculpture – that provoke a fresh perception of this historical site. Finally, Switzerland's contribution to the World Exhibition in Aichi, Japan, is an artificial mountain: a 35-m-long, 23.5-m-wide and 8.4-m-high *montagnette.* Mountain and vista are created by the artist couple Monica Studer (*1960) and Christoph van den Berg (*1962). This mountain is a quintessential symbol of what all of Switzerland and large regions of other European countries have become today: landscapes worked out to the last detail, all the way to the Alps, with viewing sites from which the landscape appears like a picture: in short, huge gardens.

Spatial cartography: in 2005 the Swiss artist Katja Schenker
created a garden artwork for the courtyard of the Federal Institute for National Topography
in Berne, Switzerland.

2006: AWARDS Switzerland's most significant landscape garden in the English style, the *Ermitage* in Arlesheim, is awarded the Schulthess-Gartenpreis, a prize established in 1998. The award honours not only the park as such – a garden first created by Balbina von Andlau-Staal (1736–1798) in 1785 and dedicated to the adulation of nature in the spirit of Jean-Jacques Rousseau, destroyed by French troops in 1793 but restored as a Romantic landscape park by Conrad von Andlau (1766–1839) in 1810–12. It also recognises and honours the restoration and conservation efforts of the current foundation "Ermitage Arlesheim und Schloss Birseck". While there have been important awards for architecture for some time – such as the Pritzker Prize to name but one – which help to elevate architects to veritable star status, prizes and awards for landscape architects are far less publicised. Thus, their gardens are often in the most literal sense in the shadow of the buildings they surround.

2006: SCULPTURE PARK V The sculpture park *Centro de Arte Contemporânea Inhotim,* planted from the mid-1980s by Brazilian businessman Bernardo de Mello Paz (*1949), opens to the public. Like its European role model, the landscape park close to the city Belo Horizonte is a gesamtkunstwerk and an educational site. With rare plants from around the world, the park becomes a huge botanical garden, and the works by internationally renowned artists placed in the landscape make it an open-air museum. On the grounds, with a design influenced by Roberto Burle Marx, among others, are twenty-three pavilions in which artworks are exhibited. In addition, at *Inhotim,* transdisciplinary courses are held for schools on art, botany and biodiversity as well as sustainable development. On a walk (or on a drive in an open electric bus), visitors experience a balance of lush nature and expressive art.

2008: BIODIVERSITY The Svalbard Global Seed Vault opens on Spitsbergen, Norway. Sunk into permafrost, the bunker is able to house around 4.5 million seed samples of 500 seeds each from around the world. The goal is to protect genetic species diversity, which ultimately means, nutritional security. The first request for a return

Contemporary art in tropical nature: *Centro de Arte Contemporânea Inhotim*, Brazil

of seeds to the arid regions areas near Aleppo, Syria, arrives in
September 2015.

2009: URBAN GARDENING III U.S. First Lady Michelle
Obama (*1964) causes a furore with her organic vegetable garden in
the park of the White House in Washington D.C. The garden is part
of her mission to battle fast food and obesity and also provides the
presidential table with vegetables, herbs, lettuce and flowers. Although
acting here as role model, it has long been an important movement:
in many countries, the economic and financial crises have led people
to plant their own gardens again and revive knowledge of gardening.
In major cities such as Detroit, residents turn wasteland into vegetable
gardens, and in Iceland, after the collapse of the banking system, the
vegetable garden is suddenly seen as a possibility for self-help.

Numerous community gardens also emerge in middle-class neighbourhoods, such as *Prinzessinnengarten* in Berlin (since 2009), planted in raised compost beds; people want to plant on free spaces and
create a meeting place, a new Arcadia. Projects such as *The Endless
Orchard* in Los Angeles ("Planted by the public, for the public, ...
a living public artwork that anyone can eat from!") and *Windy City
Harvest Youth Farm* in Chicago, represent the growing interest in
local and community food production, local consumption, as well
as social and political involvement. For aimless youth, former prison-
ers and refugees, the garden becomes a place where they can find
grounding (again).

At any rate, in an era of dense structures, "urban green" signifies
more than simply compensation areas or free space, but also self-
subsistence, encounter and social work. Also the in-part intercultural
garden projects in Switzerland, such as the *Stadiongarten Zürich*, Urban Agriculture Netz Basel's garden and *Plantages* in Lausanne, which
was awarded the Schulthess-Gartenpreis in 2015 by the Swiss Heritage
Society, show that it is possible to live a social utopia with small-scale
gardening.

2009: PUBLIC PARKS IX The first section of the *High Line
Park* in New York by the Dutch landscape architect Piet Oudolf is

opened to the public. | The disused elevated railway track in Manhattan rebuilt as a green space is finally completed in 2014. The importance of every tiny bit of green space grows in relation to the density of development, which can lead to the upgrading of entire neighbourhoods. The *High Line Park* becomes a role model for other cities: in Vienna, *High Line Park Vienna* is planned for the railway tracks out to Heiligenstadt and the *Linear Landscapes* on the approach to Nordwestbahnhof; and in London, *Garden Bridge over the Thames* is being planned. In Zurich, the former train tracks on the Letten viaduct have been a green pedestrian and bicycle bridge since 2009, by means of which one reaches the public park *Josefswiese,* which opened in 1924 – a green oasis in the former industrial quarters.

In New York, the first underground botanical garden is meanwhile being planned: *The Lowline Park* should flourish by 2021 at the trolley terminal, decommissioned in 1948, on the Lower East Side of Manhattan near the Williamsburg Bridge. From October 2015 to February 2017 tests are carried out in the Lowline Lab to figure out how to guide sunlight into the underground station by means of mirrors, thereby making it possible to grow plants.

2009: GARDEN THERAPY II Several German, Austrian and Swiss universities and garden associations come together to found the Internationale Gesellschaft Garten-Therapie (IGGT). The healing power of walks in the garden has been recognised since classical Antiquity. From the 1970s, garden therapy is given scientific weight through the emergence of interdisciplinary research – first in America, then in Europe. Being active in sun, wind and weather, experiencing the seasons and cyclic rhythms of growth and decay, being tied to the earth, helps people gain confidence through visible results. Meanwhile, in homes for the elderly, open-air therapy rooms with *raised planting beds* – crates that elevate the beds to table height – as well as vegetable gardens, gardens to stroll through and areas planted specifically for dementia patients, are included in the recognised methods, along with garden work for treating people with fears, depression and issues with addiction.

Small and large gardens invigorate the landscape: pot garden in Kanazawa, Japan

2012: RESTORATION IV The *Shalamar Gardens* in Lahore, Pakistan, from 1637 joins the *Red List of Unesco World Heritage sites,* because the surrounding wall among other features and the nearly 400-year-old irrigation system are being destroyed by the widening of a road. The walls and reservoirs have meanwhile been restored.

2013: URBAN GARDENING IV Japanese architect Ryue Nishizawa (*1966) successfully opens the house up to the garden and vice versa, bringing the garden into the house with his *Garden and House.* In Tokyo, built into a mere 4-m-wide gap between two residential towers, the minute four-storey residential home is a prime example of the merger of inside and outside, metropolitan landscape and garden nature. Plants grow in pots on every floor and continue a practice encountered throughout Japanese cities: potted gardens on the pavement in front of the door to people's homes.

2014: HANGING GARDENS V AND INSPIRATION XIII The twin residential towers *Bosco Verticale* in Milan are completed. Inspired by Italo Calvino's (1923–1985) novel *Il barone rampante* (1957, *The Baron in the Trees*), the architect Stefano Boeri (*1956) and his office design two residential buildings, 110- and 76-m high, whose facades are decorated with concrete troughs in which around 900 trees and roughly 20000 plants as well as shrubs, bushes and herbs grow. The botanist Laura Gatti together with her team at the University of Milan work out the selection of 20 different deciduous trees and conifers and the 80 other plant species. Especially challenging are the small size of the plant beds, potential high wind speeds and the water supply. Gatti and her team therefore use a wind canal to test tree species and ultimately choose the appropriate trees for planting on the facade.

Water is transported from the cellar of the building to the roof through a hose system and from there transferred to the plants. The pool in the cellar is filled with tap water from the buildings and with rainwater. With the help of a crane mounted on the roof, gardeners tightrope along the facade and tend to the plants, which are the communal property of the residents. Although the technical effort is substantial great – that is the engineering work and selection and breeding of plants – the microclimate that arises through the planting ultimately lowers the energy use of the high-rises and increases the biodiversity of the neighbourhood; some bird species have even returned to the Porta Nova district.

The *Bosco Verticale,* honoured with the Internationale Hochhauspreis der Stadt Frankfurt am Main in November 2014 and named the world's best high-rise by The Skyscraper Center of the Council on Tall Buildings and Urban Habitat in Chicago in 2015, points the way to the future with its integration of plants into the urban space. *Vertical foresting* has become a global trend. For example, the Vertical Forest Hotel is currently being planned for the Chinese city of Nanjing.

In addition, by 2020, Stefano Boeri's *Tour des Cèdres* should be completed in Chavannes-près-Renens near Lausanne. Cedars, oaks, maples and other types of trees are being bred specifically for the 117-m-high facade. The first greened residential high-rise in Switzerland, built by Buchner Bründler Architekten in 2016, is in Wabern near Berne. Here, too, nature and city, nature and architecture, come together to form a new entity.

2017: USE AND PLEASURE VI Cities and agglomerations currently continue their sprawl further and further into their surroundings; but at the same time, gardens are increasingly reconquering cities. Open green spaces emerge more on the fringes of cities, for example, as shown by *Tempelhofer Feld* in Berlin, which according to a 2014 directive must be preserved without change. Yet in centres, the small community, rooftop and courtyard gardens form an increasingly concentrated green network. The planting offers not only new living spaces for animals, such as birds and insects, but also improves the living quality for people, as plants absorb carbon dioxide and moderate noise, dust and heat and calm the soul through their poetry. The small gardens, whether horizontally around houses and on terraces and rooftops or vertically climbing up along the facades, ideally embody the motto "Think globally, act locally". They are also an expression of those initiatives that have their roots in the population, which in English are called "grassroots movements", a term closely associated with a garden.

Gardening in a time of high-density building:
Bosco Verticale in the springtime, Porta Nuova, Milan, Italy

ACKNOWLEDGEMENTS

I would like to thank all who have supported the work on this book, especially Claudio Barandun, Michael Busslinger, Anne Bürgisser, Mauricio Dias, Ursula Eichenberger, Marion Elmer, Frank Ellenberger, Nicolas Faure, Markus Gasser, Barbara Geiser, Cristina Iglesias, Alain Nicolas Lavanchy, Nicolas Olonetzky, Walter Riedweg, Katja Schenker, Christian Schmidt, Schweizerische Stiftung für Landschaftsarchitektur (SLA) Rapperswil, Pater Beda Szukics/Benediktiner-Kollegium Sarnen, Gian Vaitl, Udo and Rita Weilacher, as well as Ruth Widmer. I would also like to thank Muriel Comby and Katharina Kulke, Lisa Rosenblatt and Regula Walser for the great collaboration.

Nadine Olonetzky

SELECTED BIBLIOGRAPHY

The scope and presentation of this text did not allow for the inclusion of detailed source references. A summary of key sources follows:
Neue Jerusalemer Bibel, Einheitsübersetzung mit dem Kommentar der Jerusalemer Bibel, Herder Verlag, Freiburg 1985; M. Carroll-Spillecke (ed.), *Der Garten von der Antike bis zum Mittelalter, Kulturgeschichte der antiken Welt*, Vol. 57, Verlag Philipp von Zabern, Mainz am Rhein 1992; Anne Marie Fröhlich (ed.), *Garten – Texte aus der Weltliteratur*, Manesse Verlag, Zürich 1993; Gabrielle van Zuylen, *The Garden – Visions of Paradise*, Thames & Hudson, London 1995, reprinted 2000 and 2004; Hans Sarkowicz, *Die Geschichte der Garten und Parks*, Insel Verlag, Frankfurt am Main/Leipzig 1998; Ehrenfried Kluckert, *Gartenkunst in Europa – Von der Antike bis zur Gegenwart*, Könemann Verlag, Köln 2000; Thies Schröder, *Inszenierte Naturen – Zeitgenössische Landschaftsarchitektur in Europa*, Birkhäuser Verlag, Basel/Boston/Berlin 2001; *Jane Brown, Der moderne Garten – Gartengeschichte des 20. Jahrhunderts*, Verlag Eugen Ulmer, Stuttgart 2002; *Das Gartenbuch, Phaidon Verlag*, Berlin 2002; Udo Weilacher, *Landschaftsarchitekturführer Schweiz*, Birkhäuser Verlag, Basel/Boston/Berlin 2002; Penelope Hobhouse, *Der Garten – eine Kulturgeschichte*, Dorling Kindersley Verlag, Starnberg 2003; Gabriele Uerscheln, Michaela Kalusok, *Kleines Wörterbuch der europäischen Gartenkunst*, Reclam, Stuttgart 2003; Penelope Hill, *Contemporary History of Garden Design*, Birkhäuser Verlag, Basel/Boston/Berlin 2004; Nicholas Alfrey, Stephen Daniels, Martin Postle, *Art of the Garden – The Garden in British Art, 1800 to the Present Day*, Tate Britain/Tate Publishing, London 2004; Nadine Olonetzky, Jacqueline Schärli, *du – Zeitschrift für Kultur*, Nr. 758 – *In den Gärten. Jäten im Paradies*, Verlag Niggli, Sulgen 2005; Robert Harrison, Garten – *Ein Versuch über das Wesen der Menschen*, Carl Hanser Verlag, München 2010; Vereinigung Schweizerischer Stadtgärtnereien und Gartenbauämter (ed.), *Wert und Nutzen von Grünräumen – Literaturstudie*, VSS G, Kilchberg 2010; Nina Gerlach, *Gartenkunst im Spielfilm*, Wilhelm Fink Verlag, Paderborn 2012; Yoko Kawaguchi, *Japanische Zen-Garten – Wege zur Kontemplation*, DVA, München 2014; Albert Lutz, *Garten der Welt*, Museum Rietberg Zürich, Wienand Verlag, Köln 2016; Köbi Gantenbein, Raimund Rodewald, *Arkadien – Landschaften poetisch gestalten*, Edition Hochparterre, Zurich 2016; Marion Löhndorf, «Hinter jedem Garten liegt das Paradies», in: *Neue Zürcher Zeitung*, 8. September 2016; Annemarie Bucher, Claudia Moll, Johannes Stoffler, «Querbeet – Entdeckungen und Lehreiches aus der Gartenwelt», *Topiari helvetica* 2017 – Zeitschrift der SGGK; *Hanbury Botanischer Garten*, Brochure of the University of Genoa; *Der Weg der Alpen in die Gärten und Landschaften Europas* – Exhibition of the Verband Schweizerischer Gärtnermeister

198

(VSG), www.gtla.hsr.ch/fileadmin/user_upload/gtla.hsr.ch/AS LA/Ausstellung_Der_
Weg_der_Alpen.pdf; William Blake, http://www.gedichte.vu/?the_garden_of_love.
html.

PICTURE CREDIT

akg-images: p. 16/17, 22, 27, 32, 41, 50, 54, 81, 124
Erich Lessing / akg-images: p. 34
Hilbich / akg-images: p. 103
Jost Schilgen / akg-images: p. 77
Pirozzi / akg-images: p. 38
Rabatti-Domingie / akg-images: p. 75
Sotheby's / akg-images: p. 98
Bildarchiv Florian Monheim / akg-images: p. 66, 87, 132
British Library / akg-images: p. 52
The Bridgeman Art Library: p. 78, 142
Biblioteca Estense, Modena / The Bridgeman Art Library: p. 73
The Stapleton Collection / The Bridgeman Art Library: p. 36, 82, 122
Yale Center for British Art, Paul Mellon Collection, USA / The Bridgeman
    Art Library: p. 59
Victoria & Albert Museum London / The Bridgeman Art Library: p. 42, 58
Nick Meers / National Trust Picture Library: p. 96
Andrew Butler / National Trust Picture Library: p. 91
David Sellman / National Trust Picture Library: p. 153
G. Simeone / Huber Images: p. 47
Alessandro Della Bella / Keystone: p. 107
Boris Roessler / Keystone: p. 183
Achim Bednorz: p. 56
Benediktiner-Kollegium Sarnen: 70/71
Anne Bürgisser: p. 167
Michael Busslinger: p. 4/5, 8/9, 25, 64, 110/111, 134, 136, 191, 210/211
Frank Lorin Ellenberger: p. 10
Nicolas Faure: p. 177
Jeffery Howe: p. 151
Alain Nicolas Lavanchy: p. 154, 162, 168, 174, 175
Rémy Markowitsch / Courtesy Galerie Eigen+Art, Berlin: p. 84
Nadine Olonetzky: cover, p. 1, 2/3, 6/7, 37, 61, 63, 68, 69, 89, 92, 100, 109, 112/113,
    114/115, 116/117, 118/119, 126, 127, 128, 131, 139, 141, 144, 156, 172, 180, 184, 186,
    194, 208/209,
212/213, 214/215, 216
Nicolas Olonetzky: p. 105, 148
Katja Schenker: p. 189
Martha Schwartz Inc.: p. 165
Schweizerische Stiftung für Landschaftsarchitektur SLA, Rapperswil: p. 159
Abbey Library of St. Gall: p. 44
St. Catherines College: p. 161
Gian Vaitl: p. 197
Udo and Rita Weilacher: p. 170, 178, 179

Garden of the Heian-jingū Shinto shrine erected in 1895, Kyoto, Japan, and *topiary* in the *Victorian Garden* of Levens Hall, Kendal, Cumbria, England

Animals and geometric figures: topiary in *Jardim Botânico da Madeira*, Funchal, Portugal | 1885: MIXED BORDERS, IMPORT IV AND FLOATING GARDEN II

The Galeria True Rouge in the sculpture park *Centro de Arte Contemporânea Inhotim*, Brazil | 2006: SCULPTURE PARK V

In the garden of Villa Pastori, Ameno, Italy

In the *Parc de la Villette,* Paris, France | 1986: POST-MODERNISM IN FRANCE

Bed with herbaceous perennials selected according to colour and form. Private garden, England | 1885: MIXED BORDERS, IMPORT IV AND FLOATING GARDEN II

Water-lily pond in Ueno Park, Tokyo, Japan | 1848: PUBLIC PARKS V

Moss ground cover in the garden of the Nanzen-ji Zen Buddhist temple, Kyoto, Japan | 1859: CULTURAL TRANSFER VI – CHINOISERIE AND JAPONISM

In front of the entrance to the *Vegetation Room Inhotim* (2010–2012), a labyrinthine sculpture by the Spanish artist Cristina Iglesias, *Centro de Arte Contemporânea Inhotim*, Brazil | 2006: SCULPTURE PARK V

The *Jardín de cactus* by the artist César Manrique, Guatiza, Lanzarote, Spain | 1990: CACTUS GARDEN

Pond in the garden of the Heian-jingū Shinto shrine erected in 1895, Kyoto, Japan | 1859: CULTURAL TRANSFER VI – CHINOISERIE AND JAPONISM

Private pot garden at a street intersection, Rio de Janeiro, Brazil

—

Private garden on the island of Teshima, Japan

Studio and home of the artists Mauricio Dias and Walter Riedweg, Santa Teresa, Rio de Janeiro, Brazil

Jardim Botânico da Madeira with a view over Funchal and the Atlantic, Madeira, Portugal | 1885: MIXED BORDERS, IMPORT IV AND FLOATING GARDEN II

Small greenhouse with succulents, private garden, England | 1876: GREENHOUSE II

In the garden of Villa Pastori, Ameno, Italy

INDEX NAMES

INDEX PLACES

205

IMPRINT

This book is based in part on the text "Sensations of European Garden History – A chronologial collection of keywords", which was published in issue 758 – "In the Gardens. Weeding in Paradise" – of the cultural journal *du* in 2005. It is also a completely revised and comprehensively expanded new edition of the book *Sensations – A Time Travel through Garden History,* which was published by Birkhäuser Verlag in 2006.

Nadine Olonetzky was born in Zurich in 1962. She writes on subjects in the fields of photography, art and cultural history and has authored and edited several books. She is a member of *Kontrast* (www.kontrast.ch), a project director/editor with the publishers Scheidegger & Spiess and lives in Zurich.

Picture Editing: Nadine Olonetzky
Translation from German into English:
Lisa Rosenblatt, Elisabeth Schwaiger
Copy editing: Keonaona Peterson
Project management: Katharina Kulke
Production: Heike Strempel
Editorial Design: Muriel Comby

Paper: Fly 06, 130g/m²
Printing: Kösel GmbH & Co. KG,
Altusried-Krugzell

Library of Congress Cataloging-in-Publication data
A CIP catalogue record for this book has been applied for at the Library of Congress.

Bibliographic information published by the German National Library
The German National Library lists this publication in the Deutsche Nationalbibliografie; detailed bibliographic data are available on the Internet at http://dnb.dnb.de.

This publication is also available in a German language edition (ISBN 978-3-7643-7622-2).

© 2017 Birkhäuser Verlag GmbH, Basel
P.O. Box 44, 4009 Basel, Switzerland
Part of Walter de Gruyter GmbH, Berlin/Boston

Printed on acid-free paper produced from chlorine-free pulp. TCF ∞

Printed in Germany
ISBN 978-3-7643-7623-9

9 8 7 6 5 4 3 2 1
www.birkhauser.com